Undertones
Mild Mysticism in an Age of Umber

Undertones
Mild Mysticism in an Age of Umber

Dick Sullivan

Coracle Books

By the same author:

Prose
Old ships
Navvyman

Poetry
Capperbar
Melanie
The Moon at Midnight
Morning on the Mountain

For more about these books, and also work in progress, readers are invited to visit the author's website and blog: **www.ageofumber.com**.

ISBN 978 0 906280 98 0

For Mary

Foreword

This book was suggested by a series of essays I wrote for www.Victorianweb.org. Slowly the theme of the book emerged – the fact that a strain of mysticism has run through English art and literature for centuries, though today this is barely recognised or even understood. That being so, I would especially like to thank George P Landow, Professor of English and Art History at Brown University for publishing them on his VW website. The opinions expressed here are, of course, entirely mine, as are any errors, mistakes, or misreadings. Professor Landow showed scholarly tolerance, not approval.

Dick Sullivan
London, 2010

Contents

To Begin With ...

One Spring morning some time ago a four year old boy was taken for a walk on the hills. Against the sky he saw a briar bush. All at once he was filled with a strange and rather terrible joy verging on ecstasy. This experience, of course, was new to him but as the years came and went so did similar encounters, sometimes frequently, sometimes less so. He accepted it all as part of life, although he always thought it a bit odd that nobody ever spoke about these strange things. Nobody did and it was a very long time before he realised they were a watered down version of what the great mystics experienced. In other words, they were 'spiritual'.

Being an agnostic, the boy – now a middle-aged man – didn't link them to a God of any kind. Instead they invoked a feeling of a stillness, peace, purity and simplicity underlying all creation. In time he realised it could be also called Love. Was he a mystic? If he were it could only be of a lower, lesser, minor, semi- or common kind. 'Common' because he thought he couldn't be alone in this. If he hadn't made the connection for half a century, perhaps millions of others never made the connection at all? (And if nobody had ever spoken about these odd encounters, neither had he.) By now he also knew what caused them: it's what happens when thought and thinking is, very briefly, stopped. It's as automatic and simple as that. That mental shut down is triggered by many things – art, physical love, love, landscape, patriotism, even thought itself can be so overwhelming it shuts itself down.

The mystic moment is brief – lasting only seconds very often – but it seems like a sudden gift of sight. The outcome is joy, or undiluted happiness. This is so invariable it can be used as a test; without it the experience is spurious. Another check is: 'Does what has happened make you bigger and better?' If it doesn't, it's fake. The mystic vision, minor or otherwise, is always free of hate, envy, spite, discontent and always associated with joy and love. It imparts a feeling that life has a point and a purpose. It's life-developing, life-enlarging, life-building.

Alongside these encounters was something harder to pin down. There seemed to be something nameless working away in the unconscious mind lifting and expanding life, making it more fulfilled, more fully human, closer to the supreme simplicity of that Love which floods in when thought is shut down. What could he call these nameless energies? In the end he hit on undertones, or overtones, or an extra-meaning which surrounds ideas, landscape, words, art, music like an active halo.

Two routes are open to the lesser mystic. Stop thinking and see the underlying simplicity below common reality (or so it seems).Or fill the mind with knowledge, ideas and – more especially – undertones. For the mystically inclined the well-filled mind raises the Underlying closer to the surface of consciousness as a permanent underpresence or steady-state sub-mysticism. If the mind is reasonably poised, unpoisoned by bitterness or resentment it is there all the time, a bedrock

But is any of this true? It's certainly a fact, recordable by brain scan. Whether it's just a trick of the brain is unknowable. More importantly, it's life-lifting and not life-lowering. It's also a part of human nature, not super-nature. So why not accept it? Particularly as both undertones and mild mysticism are easy for Darwinists to accept – they may once have conferred an evolutionary advantage; without them a newly self-conscious species would have been lost on an alien world. A shut-down mind gives a sense of meaning and belonging. Undertones do likewise in a more permanent and slow-release kind of way.

Is a deeper spiritual meaning unlikely? The spiritual is really no odder than the fact of being – which is the oddest thing imaginable. Thought is the only thing you can be sure exists. Not even an 'I' to do the thinking can be proved. But thought when stilled brings about a contact with timeless simplicity. Similarly, even if you argue that matter is all that exists, immaterial thought arises from it and this thought too, when stilled, settles into unchanging peace.

Yet is it really open to all? It should be because the experience automatically follows mental shut-down. Introverts, on the other hand, are perhaps more receptive – if (that is) they're defined as people whose inner world is more real than the outer. The more inward looking the mind, the more mystical it's likely to be.

By now the boy was an old man. The last question he faced was how to explain all this to other people, few or many, who might be interested in such things? Slowly he became aware that history is alive with minor mystics; for centuries they'd been artists, composers, and poets – enough to fill a short book, now duly written and presented here.

Encounters of a Lesser Kind

William James (1842-1910), the American philosopher and psychologist, also thought most people have a 'mystical germ'. He had one himself. As with so many things, there are degrees of mysticism, from high through medium to low. His book, *The Varieties of Religious Experience* (1902), is a series of case studies of everyday mysticism, mainly of the second and third levels. Of himself he said the feeling was faint, vague, indefinite, yet without it there'd be "a great hush, a great void in my life." It was like a tune at the back of the mind, just beyond recall. The experience, he concluded, is indescribable: it's more than an emotion (it's an enlightenment), it's quick, it's brief, it's a gift. A sense of harmony and joy is *always* the outcome.

Frederick Happold, one time headmaster of Bishop Wordsworth's Grammar School in Salisbury, had three mystical experiences and wrote several books on the strength of them. What happened to him, he realised, was different only in degree and not in kind from the mysticism of people like St Paul. Paul was major, Happold was minor, both were mystics.

In 1913 he was still an undergraduate in Peterhouse in Cambridge when the first event occurred in his room late one evening. A red shaded lamp stood on the table. The furnishings were shabby. He became aware of a Presence and felt an immeasurable joy which lasted into the next day. Three years later, now an infantry officer, he was crouching in a crater filled with mud and corpses waiting to lead his platoon over the top. It was the Battle of the Somme. "And suddenly with absolute certainty, I knew that I was utterly safe." The third event happened twenty years later. His first child had been still-born. He was anxious because his wife was about to give birth again. Then, suddenly while lying in bed, complete peace came over him and he saw there was a pattern into which all things, including himself, were woven. The weaver was Love.

Happold also quotes from John Buchan's autobiography, *Memory Hold-the-Door*. Buchan (1875-1940) was an unlikely mystic: he's best known now as a thriller-writer (of *The Thirty-nine Steps* in particular) and novelists rarely seem to be mystical. On top of that he was a man of action involved in imperial, if not global, politics. He was the oldest son of a minister of the Wee Free Kirk, a Grammar School boy and an Oxford graduate who, in the early years of the 20th century, became a colonial official in South Africa. (Not a lowly one: he was private secretary to Lord Milne, Governor of Cape Colony and later High Commissioner in South Africa.) In the Great War he was a subaltern but not in the front line because of his age: instead, he was an Intelligence officer and speech writer for Field Marshal Haig, C-in-C British Expeditionary Force. Later, as Lord Tweedsmuir, Buchan served as Governor-General of Canada. He died there of a stroke while shaving one morning in 1940. In his autobiography, published that same year, he recalled a time when as a young man he was trekking in the Kalahari Desert:

"I had been ploughing all day in the black dust of the Lichtenburg roads, and had come very late to a place called he eye of the Malmani – Malmani Oog – the spring of a river which presently loses itself in the Kalahari. We watered our horses and went supperless to bed. Next morning I bathed in one of the Malmani pools – and icy cold it was – and then basked in the early sunshine while breakfast was cooking. The water made a pleasant music, and near by was a covert of willows filled with singing birds. Then and there came on me the hour of revelation, when, though savagely hungry, I forgot about breakfast. Scents, sights, and sounds blended into a harmony so perfect that it transcended human expression, even human thought. It was like a glimpse of the peace of eternity."

Among the more expected mystical poets (Blake, Wordsworth, Shelley, Keats, Browning) Happold also includes John Masefield (1878-1967). Masefield was the son of solicitor of Ledbury in Herefordshire. When his mother died he went to live with an aunt who sent him to the naval training ship *Conway* in the River Mersey to stop him reading so much. In the 1890s he rounded the Horn in the barque *Gilcruix* on passage to Chile, from where he was sent home by steamer suffering from sun stroke and a nervous breakdown. Judging by the sensitivity of his face in his portraits he was an unlikely seaman, particularly one sailing before the mast and living in the rough and tumble of the fo'c's'le. His aunt thought otherwise; she sent him to join a Windjammer in New York (he was still a minor, aged only seventeen). He seems to have jumped ship before he was even signed on and became a hobo, a barman, and then a carpet weaver. Back in England he married a woman a few years older than himself and they stayed happily together until she died, aged ninety, in 1960. In the Great War he served with the RAMC as an orderly both on the Western Front, and then in charge of the ambulance boats at Gallipoli in the Dardanelles. Post-War he kept bees and goats on Boar's Hill in the Cumnor Hills across the river from Oxford. More importantly he had a private theatre in his garden for plays and poetry recitals. He also set up the Oxford Recitations to promote the art of verse speaking. On top of that he was Poet Laureate for thirty years – one of only three mystically inclined laureates (the others being Wordsworth and Tennyson).

Three years before the Great War he'd written *The Everlasting Mercy*, a long poem about redemption through mysticism. It's of its time but with some beautiful descriptions of nature as seen through a mystic's eyes. Saul Kane (is that Paul rising out of Cain?) is a poacher, seducer, drunk, liar, and all round wastrel. Redemption comes through a mystical experience triggered by a confrontation with an old Quaker lady. He says:

16

O glory of the lighted mind.
How dead I'd been, how dumb, how blind.
The station brook, to my new eyes,
Was babbling out of Paradise,
The waters rushing from the rain
Were singing Christ has risen again.
I thought all earthly creatures knelt
From rapture of the joy I felt.
The narrow station-wall's brick ledge,
The wild hop withering in the hedge,
The lights in huntsmans' upper storey
Were parts of an eternal glory,
Were God's eternal garden flowers.
I stood in bliss at this for hours.

Later he also says:

Out of the mist into the light,
O blessed gift of inner sight.

Although Masefield never, of course, used the words sub-mysticism or 'undertones' he clearly knew what they were: he describes them quite clearly in his 1910 poem, Fragments. Fragment are undertones which lodge in the mind to create a 'city in the soul' when something great has gone from the earth. Troy and her towers have fallen, for example, but Homer's epic lives on in the mind to make life fuller and better.

So that, when Troy had greatly passed
In one red roaring fiery coal,
The courts the Grecians overcast
Became a city in the soul.

Similarly with Plato's Atlantis (and the myths that have grown up around it since). The Atlanteans, Masefield says:

... knew all wisdom, for they knew
The souls of those Egyptian Kings
Who learned, in ancient Babilu,
The beauty of immortal things.

Because they knew immortal beauty their thoughts struck the air like music from lyre strings before being turned into golden birds of fire which perch in the foliage of the heart. This may be a bit overwrought in prose, though not so much in poetry:

> They knew all beauty – when they thought
> The air chimed like a stricken lyre,
> The elemental birds were wrought,
> The golden birds became a fire.
>
> And straight to busy camps and marts
> The singing flames were swiftly gone;
> The trembling leaves of human hearts
> Hid boughs for them to perch upon.

But although Atlantis has gone, the undertones – the fragments – live on as a city in the soul:

> The dream that fires man's heart to make,
> To build, to do, to sing or say
> A beauty Death can never take,
> An Adam from the crumbled clay.

He had his own personal fragments or undertones, of course. Many of them were those of a Victorian boy – buccaneers on the Spanish Main, wine in taverns by tropical seas: hornpipes, palms and pirates, silver flagons and gold doubloons. They lasted, if not for life (and probably they did – they usually do) at least well in his young adulthood when he wrote so many poems with similar themes. Often there's a tinge of melancholy and sadness about them which, as we'll see later, is vital to the semi-mystical way of looking at things.

First there were the good times, the days of yore when carefree sailormen danced barefoot on deck or on the sanded floors of taverns by the sea:

> With the silver seas around us and the pale moon
>   overhead.
> And the look-out not a-looking and his pipe-bowl
>   glowing red.

The good times rolled until bureaucracy in the shape of the grey-souled Board of Trade took the colour out of life, though leaving the undertones or fragments behind, to make the spirit less mean and spiteful.

The schooners and the merry crews are laid away to rest
A little south the sunset in the Islands of the Blest.

In cases like these, of course, the undertones don't reflect reality. But reality is beside the point. Masefield knew the reality of life before the mast. In his book, *Sea Life in Nelson's Time* (1905), he says: "Man is always ready to ignore the pounds of misery and squalor which go to make each pennyweight of glory." Many people in this early 21st century West ignore the pennyweight and look only for the squalor. Both are real, albeit at either end of a spectrum, and one – the pennyweight of glory – is abstract. Out of an abstraction, though, the mind can make its own life-increasing fragments.

Buchan and Masefield (and Happold) were second tier mystics of the mild, minor, lesser kind. Not many at this level, you'd think, can change the world, except locally. Big changes are surely made by big mystics? In her book, *Mystics of the Church* (1925), Evelyn Underhill argues that what people think of as St Paul's theology was in reality his 'desperate attempts' to describe the mystic experience itself – "the peace which passeth all understanding." What happened to him on the road to Damascus was a massive spiritual event which, given his importance as one of the founders of Christianity, shaped the world. Even so and in spite of it, most of the high flying mystics in history have been little more than sports, and of limited effect. Of what importance are Eckhart, Boehme or St Teresa now? Lesser and lower flying mystics – Ruskin, for example – have done much more.

THREE

Mild Mysticism and Change

John Ruskin (1819-1900) is a strangely forgotten man. Strangely because he helped to change the world in several ways – in art, politics, and how society is run. Between the ages of twenty-four and forty-one he wrote eleven books – *Modern Painters I-V*, *The Seven Lamps of Architecture*, *The Stones of Venice I-III* and *Unto This Last* – each of which had an impact on the world from the way people look at paintings, to the Gothic Revival, to the Welfare State.

He was born a mystic and remained one, actively and untaught, until his thirties. Mysticism for him began as soon as his brain had grown enough to register things. At the age of four or five his nurse took him to Friar's Crag above Derwentwater in Westmorland. Years later he recalled the "intense joy, mingled with awe, I had in looking through the hollows in the mossy roots, over the crag, into the dark lake." What he called his 'destiny' was fixed by another spiritual experience at the age of fourteen when, from a terrace above the Rhine, he saw the Alps in the far distance like the rose-tinted walls of Eden. Another (one of many) experience came to him, in his mid-twenties, in the Chamonix valley in Switzerland. A thunder storm raged below the high, serene, unmoved, sunlit, peaks which were "the very heart of heaven – a celestial city with walls of amethyst and gates of gold – filled with the light and clothed with the Peace of God." For the first time he really understood beauty. To see it you must "turn the human soul from gazing upon itself". "It was only then I understood that to become nothing might be to become more than Man."

In this he discovered for himself the trick of the mystic:

20

switch off thought. Elsewhere he quotes Wordsworth who realised the same thing:

> In such high hour
> Of visitation from the living God
> *Thought* was not.

Similarly, Ruskin also saw that repose is at the heart of all great art; at its centre is always stillness. This is Plato's Being, as opposed to the Becoming of the daily round. It's Parmenides's theory that nothing changes, as opposed to Heraclitus who believed the cosmos is nothing but change ("you can't step into the same river twice"). Together they add up to the mystic vision: the fact that unchangingness underlies change.

Landscape, more particularly high mountainous landscape, triggered Ruskin's mystic moments. "The one who loves nature most," he wrote, "will *always* be found to have more *faith* in God than the other." And: "nature-worship ... becomes the channel to sacred truth, which by no other means can be conveyed." Through these insights Ruskin made the connection between beauty and the divine. Beautiful things, for him, were like windows through which he could see what he called God, though he realised it went deeper than organised religion: the vision is primary while what you make of it is cultural – a Zen roshi watching that Alpine storm would never have thought of a god at all.

Great ages are spiritual, he claimed, and so is great art. Great art also needs a cohesive society. The Middle Ages had both. Out of a wholeness of life, work, and the spiritual came the great Cathedrals, the immaterial encased in stone. "All great Art is Praise," he wrote in the Epilogue to *Modern Painters* long after his mystic days were over. Art, like all things spiritual, is inconsistent with spite and discontent. Always it's about love and joy. Art is the embodiment of a civilisation. This, in turn, means that society's failings can't be hidden. If a society is bad and ugly so will its art be, for all to see.

Medieval Venice, in particular, showed this blending of the spiritual and the everyday, and what happens when the connection is broken. The fall from Gothic grace into Renaissance corruption can be traced in the city's art and architecture (the stones) as it collapsed into an 'insolent atheism' which raised people above God. The freedom of the Medieval workman was replaced by a fixity of rules and blueprints. Wholeness was betrayed. Ruskin worried, not without reason (or prescience), that it could happen to England. He called the 19th century the Age of Umber and thought the darkness of the times was caused by a lack of faith, or the loss of a wholeness of outlook and life. Where the Greeks saw gods in the woods, the Victorians saw poachers; where the Middle Ages saw angels in clouds, the Victorians predicted rain.

He began his career by expounding Turner to the English in *Modern Painters I*. Classicist artists like Claude and Poussin painted landscapes which had never been seen (or see-able) on earth. Turner, on the other hand, saw nature as it really is and painted what he saw. Great art reveals God, Ruskin thought, because beauty is a sign of Divinity. If Beauty controls morals, then its absence brings about moral and emotional decay. If Beauty comes in through the eye, then people have to be taught to look. How? Through awareness of detail. Examples of what he meant can be taken almost at random from *Modern Painters* – Turner's water fall in Upper Teesdale, for instance. Foam is easy to fake, Ruskin claimed; scuffing the paper lightly is one way, crumbling white paint on it another. A leap of water is not hard to do, either. But what Turner paints is the 'tumble' of water – its unhindered drop from rock lip to pool. Turner catches not just the laciness but also the permanent patterns made by freely falling water. This is the stuff of small-time mysticism.

Furthermore, in the bigger fall to the left Turner catches the sheer force of falling water: you can almost feel the up-draught of displaced air, smell the river scent. Turner has also caught exactly the bouncing line of water where fall and pool meet. Two fishermen wade thigh deep, one with a net, one with a rod. But this isn't just photographic copying of detail. It carries a charge. Look at it and the mind will slow till it's calm enough for a sighting of something deeper and more fundamental, closer to a common mystic moment. The reality of hardship in the fishermen's lives is there yet there's also an undertone of something deeper – of mankind pitted against an elemental landscape. Two realities are caught here; hardship and elevation. It's a kind of daily bread mysticism.

Natural colour is important, too. To show its misuse Ruskin chose a painting in the National Gallery in London – Salvator Rosa's Mercury and the dishonest woodman. The background mountains are blue but detailed (you can see the crags and the cracks in the rock) although in nature any mountain distant enough to look blue will also be featureless. Turner never did anything so crass. Like nature herself *his* distant mountains are sapphire blue and smooth.

Beauty is not a force in itself – it merely unblocks and releases what's already there. The energy is in what is released not in what releases it. It's like a tool to uncap a well and let the oil gush out – the energy's in the well driving the oil, not what lifts the lid. Ruskin saw this, too; the effect of the beautiful on the mind is involuntary. He argued, against the Romantics, that what matters is the observed, not the observer. The spectator is passive. When he wrote the first volumes of Modern Painters he was still an Evangelical steeped in the Bible. He quotes from the Sermon on the Mount: "Blessed are the pure in heart, for they shall see God." This is a cultural layer laid on top of what is, in fact, the right insight: for purity of heart read being free of hate, spite, and ego. The mystic vision comes with a quiet mind: resentment can never be calm enough.

Then, like many Victorians, Ruskin lost his faith. The cause was geology, not Darwin – Lyell's *Principles of Geology* had been published in 1833 when Ruskin was twenty-four. "Those dreadful hammers!" he complained. "If only the geologists would let me alone!" The earth is very old, Lyell had discovered: in the Bible it's very very young. The final split came suddenly in a Waldensian chapel in Turin in 1858. The preacher, 'a little squeaking idiot', told his congregation (seventeen old women, 'three louts', and Ruskin) that they were only people in the city who were saved. Moments before Ruskin had been looking at Veronese's lusty *Queen of Sheba*. The contrast between the painter's largeness of mind and the bitter smallness of the preacher was too much. Besides which, Evangelical Protestantism was a strange cult for a mystic to belong to, resting as it does on the literal meaning of words first spoken in Antiquity and in other tongues. (Matthew Arnold homed in on this a few years later in his Bible criticism.) Ruskin later regained a belief of some – non-mystical? – kind.

By then he'd turned to politics, taking with him the deepest thing he knew – the fact that underlying the complexity of worldly things is a timeless simplicity. In *Modern Painters V* he argued that all great works of art are unified and whole in themselves, each obeying the universal 'Law of Help', or cooperation. In 1860 he published *Unto This Last* which argues that society should also obey the same law and that people should stop competing with each other. His ideas form the basis of the Welfare State and the basis of his ideas were mystic.

If he thought any of this was Darwinian he was wrong: the top dog and the alpha male always get to breed more often than the lower dog or deltas. Competition is built in and is relentless. Random selection means some animals are born better fitted to compete and therefore to evolve into more effective species. What Ruskin argued for was statism. Turn of the century socialists – Wilde, Shaw, Wells, Morris – all thought statism would set people free. It was, of course, the innocence of a pre-Holocaust, pre-Gulag, generation.

Ruskin's father was a sherry salesman. In other words, he was in Trade, like the village baker – although fortified wine was more profitable than bread: sherry made the Ruskins millionaires in today's money. The younger Ruskin inherited, gave most of it away, then earned another fortune through royalties. He wasn't so lucky in love and probably died a virgin. His wife Effie said he was impotent. He said he wasn't. Effie, left him for Millais. Then, Ruskin became fixated on a child, Rose la Touche, who was herself (by some accounts) unhinged by religiosity. When she was old enough, he proposed. She said no, repeatedly, and in any case died young and insane. It all helped tip Ruskin into his own bouts of madness and visions (delirious, this time, and not mystical). More famously, he was sued for libel by Whistler after Ruskin accused him of asking two hundred guineas "for throwing a pot of paint in the public's face." Whistler won a farthing in damages. (Ironically, some of Whistler's *Nocturnes* are quite good enough to invoke a milder kind of mysticism in some people, though obviously not in Ruskin.)

Given all this, it's strange that Ruskin's now nearly forgotten. Being a founder-thinker of the Welfare State is no small thing. Neither is teaching a country how to look at art. He was helpful, to say the least, to the Pre-Raphaelites. The Aesthetic Movement was a reaction, in part, to his piety, though how people like Pater and Wilde failed to see that art leads on to something deeper than itself is hard to understand – Art for Art's sake just isn't enough: there's more to life than that. More positively, if misguidedly, William Morris – the atheist socialist millionaire – started up the Arts and Crafts Movement to revive Ruskin's vision of the Middle Ages. Trade unionists read him and his ideas were taken up by the early Labour Party and the National Trust.

The Welfare State's still a reality, and the National Trust is England's second biggest landowner. What else is left of Ruskin? For the mildly mystically inclined his ideas are valuable undertones. The idea, for example, that absorbing art via a quietened mind opens up the spiritual. Or that stillness and repose are at the centre of all great art and that art is a touchstone for a society's health and well-being. It can go further: good manners are aesthetic and like all aesthetic things lead to the divine (however defined). Or what about: art fails when removed from its sacred roots? Or art like prayer communicates with God, teaching us about the unknowable (unknowable to the reasoning mind, that is)? Modern art is a kind of anxiety. An artist should be a metaphysician attaching society to the spiritual? Or that the absence of all these things makes for an Age of Umber?

FOUR

Ruskin: Romsey Abbey and the Renaissance

Is Gothic spiritually right, Renaissance wrong as Ruskin claimed? Ludgate Hill in London is named after King Lud, a pagan who probably never lived. The Gothic St Paul's cathedral which crowned it burned down in the Great Fire of 1666. Wren's replacement is very late Renaissance, just pre-Baroque in fact, all smooth marble and an echoing dome. Building began only fifteen years after the Royal Society was set up. Newton laid down the laws of motion and gravity twelve years into its building. Locke's work on the limits of human understanding, the founding document of the Enlightenment, came out when it was exactly one-quarter built. The Industrial Revolution was under way – the Bank of England was already up and running and steam engines were pumping out Cornish copper mines. A year after the cathedral was finished, Steele began writing *The Tatler* and then, with Addison, *The Spectator* – two magazines which between them helped to spread the ethos of the new Age of Reason throughout the country.

Romsey Abbey by the River Test in Hampshire is well over a thousand years old. Alfred the Great's grand-daughter was the first abbess. Years earlier, St Boniface (who converted Germany) had lived nearby in the same county, centuries before the French 'comté' part-displaced the native Anglo-Saxon 'shire'. In the late 10th century the abbey came under the rules of St Benedict. A stone rood or cross sprouting like a tree in Spring survives from that time, along with a wall and another crucifix. Today's church was built on top of the Anglo-Saxon one. Building it took from the early 12th to the late 13th centuries, mainly because the money ran out half way through. The church, therefore, is Norman or Romanesque with Gothic add-ons.

Romsey is only a few miles from Winchester, England's one time capital city: armies, politics, and kings therefore came to the abbey, and went. The abbey educated Henry I's wife, Edith. William Rufus wanted to marry her but an aunt threw a veil over the girl, claiming she was already a nun, leaving her unwed (and no nun) for Henry to take. King Stephen's daughter was abbess when Henry II mounted the throne and married her off to a friend, thus sparking the rows with Thomas à Beckett which ended in murder and sainthood many years later.

Time is an undertone and is still a living thing in the old part of town around the abbey church where Edward I's knights left graffiti on walls. A very English tea shop is now housed in a brick built Medieval kitchen. Venison from the New Forest has given way to carrot cake (home made) but you can sense the presence of a greasy scullion is in the scullery somewhere behind the great fire place.

Along with all the other nunneries, priories and monasteries, the abbey was closed down at the Dissolution. The church was saved because it was the parishioners' place of worship too. One of the last nuns, Jane Seymour's niece, married the last chaplain and their daughter in turn married into the family of the new owners of the abbey estates – which in time circulated through the hands of the Palmerston family (including the Prime Minister who championed gun boats) and the Mountbattens. Lord Louis, cousin of Queen Elizabeth II and the last Viceroy of India, was killed in a boat off Ireland by the IRA. "History has many cunning passages," as Eliot said.

Altogether it's quite a story – with other odd by-passages thrown in: Roundhead troops, for example, wrecked the church organ and a little later an apple tree grew in pigeon dung on the roof, the place was so neglected. A Victorian vicar called Berthon invented a foldaway canvas lifeboat (cobblers stitched it together). The barrel roof installed by the Victorians threatened to split the building in two until 20th century engineers put in rods to hold the walls together.

But what of the stones? The face of a master mason called

Robert is carved on a pillar – hardly a likeness, more like a cartoon of a Hallowe'en pumpkin without the candle. Forty or so other pillars have carvings on the capitals – one of Alfred the Great's last great battle in the west. These carvings are Medieval. The reredos behind the high altar looks Medieval but in fact was the last painting made in this church before the Catholics lost control of it. The abbey was still Benedictine (it had been for six hundred years) and the painting shows the founder-saint standing at the centre of a line of holy men. Below them, Christ, dressed in crimson and white, steps from the tomb flanked by Roman soldiers (astonishment is accurately painted in their faces). A nun with a shapely nose and rosy cheeks gazes rapturously upwards. Her eyes are perfectly caught, not an easy thing to do. The painting as a whole carries an undertone of serenity.

A portrait on a nearby wooden panel was painted a century earlier. A tonsured priest kneels in prayer. The painting is partly crude, partly skilled. His ear is like a rock climber's carabiner and the hands are bit botched (the painter's contemporaries in Florence would have made a better job of it). But the artist caught something more important and more extraordinary – devotion; not just a devout face but devotion itself, an abstract concept made visible in paint.

The Reformation and the Puritans put a stop to painting and so Victorian stained glass comes next in time. There's a nice window-portrait of the Rev. Berthon – stern, bearded, very Victorian with neatly parted hair and granny specs which look oddly 21st century. From the 20th century there's a 1935 carving of the Madonna and Child. From the 1960s, there's an embroidered curtain redolent of the previous decade. It was daring and very modern for its time, though now badly dated: elongated nuns, knights and bishops in blue, gold, orange, and red. Christ in a red robe has a blue face.

Romsey Abbey of course is mainly pre-Gothic Romanesque with rounded, not pointed, arches. Gothic is soaring, Romsey is squat. Pointed arches carry more weight, freeing up walls to be filled with glass and therefore light. Flying buttresses let walls get thinner. Romsey Abbey is heavier, more earth-bound, but also more elemental. Doorways are like cave openings in living rock. Pillars are an uplift of stone into darkness: every rise curves over a rounded arch, bringing the eye back down to earth again. Gothic tries to carry you on up to heaven: Romanesque is too heavy (heaven is not yet).

Was Ruskin right about Gothic and the Renaissance? Is Gothic a shout of joy, as he claimed? Did people live in a wholeness of the sacred, earth, work, and art? What would Chaucer's Pardoner have to say? Or the Wife of Bath? And who can know what Robert, the master mason, felt? All you can do is ask the 21st century. Which is the more spiritual – St Paul's or Romsey Abbey church?

Romanesque is more elemental than Gothic. Weight roots it more solidly in the soil. It's from the early days of the evolution of elegance: it has grandeur but a crudity as well. If Gothic is of the sky and Romanesque of the earth, then Renaissance is of the mind. St Paul's is a thought – tidy, dust-free, smooth, spotless and polished. On the other hand, the fact that its architecture is more intellectual should be neither here nor there. Anything which closes down thought will produce the mystic experience. Except that Gothic is more likely to do so. Time alone can account for a lot of it. Eternity is an absence of time, but time is an undertone inducing a sense of it. A thousand summers come and go, changing speech, dress, diet, thoughts, ways of working, ways of going to war, but the stillness inside a Gothic cathedral or Romanesque abbey is unchanging; a meeting yet again of the changing and the unchangeable.

FIVE

The Vale of the White Horse

L ove of country can also create undertones or even stop thought and so induce a brief minor mystic experience. Nowadays this is hard to believe in an England where the whole concept of patriotism has collapsed. Nevertheless at one time, not too long ago, it was true. The reason is simple: anything benign which leads to a sense of something greater than the self will work, as will any kind of uncorrupted love. Patriotism had both (it wasn't the nationalism of fatherland, blood and race). That sense of greaterness could be so strong that men were willing to die for it. Today it seems shameful – certainly it's shame-faced and a thing for mockery. What can people now make of Rupert Brooke (the most handsome young man in England, according to W B Yeats)? Brooke had mystic experiences himself – one was triggered by the blemished skin of strangers in a train. (He died, age twenty-eight, of septicaemia from a mosquito bite on his way to Gallipoli with the Royal Naval Division in 1915.)

> If I should die, think only this of me:
> That there's some corner of a foreign field
> That is for ever England. There shall be
> In that rich earth a richer dust concealed;
> A dust whom England bore, shaped, made aware,
> Gave, once, her flowers to love, her ways to roam,
> A body of England's, breathing English air,
> Washed by the rivers, blest by suns of home.
>
> And think, this heart, all evil shed away,
> A pulse in the eternal mind, no less

Gives somewhere back the thoughts by England given,
Her sights and sounds; dreams happy as her day;
And laughter, learnt of friends; and gentleness,
In hearts at peace, under an English heaven.

This, *The Soldier*, was written in 1914 at the beginning of the Great War when patriotism was at its height. But perhaps for some of a certain intellectual cast of mind it'd begun to wane long before?

Thomas Hughes (1822-1896) published *Tom Brown's Schooldays* in 1857. In one passage he tells undergraduates not to take their holidays abroad. What were they missing at home? Wood sorrel, bog bean and battle fields. Before going overseas, he seemed to be saying, they should cultivate a sense of belonging to the country where they'd been born. Love of country, its history and landscape, would create an undertone – a place of settled strength and peace at the centre of their being: a country in the soul, to paraphrase Masefield.

Two years later Hughes picked up the theme again in his second novel, *The Scouring of the White Horse*. A London clerk is asked down to Berkshire to learn, through its history and customs, what his country stands for. In other words, to acquire undertones, if not a direct spiritual insight. On the surface, not a lot happens: country ways include cart-horse racing, cheese rolling, wine and cheesecake making. But what about below the surface? Auden coined the word 'topophilia' to describe the way John Betjeman felt about landscapes which are rooted in time. It means love of a place which has been shaped over centuries by human hands. The Vale of the White Horse fits the bill. It's small – five mile by eighteen, perhaps, with the barely visible River Ock flowing unnoticed on its way to the Thames. The hills are chalk, never quite making it to a thousand feet. The White Horse is carved near the crest – facing upwards: it was cut for gods to see, not the people of the vale, and can be seen in full only from the air. When the city clerk came here, it was dairy country with thick hedges. More corn is grown now and the elms have all gone but, outwardly, it probably hasn't changed too much, though they sell burgers and fries in the Fox and Hounds in Uffington, and the dialect is rarely Royal Berkshire.

It's also a good place for topophilia. The Ridgeway runs along the crest of the hills on its way from Dorset to Lincoln. It was a great Stone Age highway which has been walked or ridden on for five thousand years. The Victorians thought the Horse was copied from the Saxon Royal Standard. In fact it's probably Stone Age. It's a very beautiful thing – four hundred feet of sinuous, disconnected lines, an elongated outline of a galloping horse with a single enormous eye in a head sketched in by two or three brief strokes. Uffington Castle is Iron Age, and was probably the site of the Battle of Badon where King Arthur (the real one, not the man from Camelot) beat the English. Wayland's Smithy is a Stone Age grave. Wayland was the Anglo-Saxon god of smiths (copper, bronze, or black). He'll shoe your horse down to this day if you leave it tied up along with some silver. Hughes, who was born in Uffington in the Vale, knew what he was talking about. Many a time he must have stood up there by the oldest road in England (in Europe?) looking down on the steam trains of the Great Western Railway trailing smoke along the floor of the Vale; the oldest and the newest with, as he supposed, one of the world's most important battles in between.

This is because the Victorians mistakenly thought the Vale of the White Horse was the site of King Alfred's great battle against the Danes, in 878, which saved England for the English, and thus changed the whole direction of the world. If he'd lost, the earth would be a very different place. No English language as we know it. No Norman Conquest, no Shakespeare, Common Law, Enlightenment, (no USA), no Industrial Revolution. Scholars may dispute these things nowadays, and probably do (they dispute everything else), though the Butterfly Effect alone suggests everything would be very different.

That battle took place, in fact, at Ethandune, today's Edington, in Wiltshire. From the point of view of sub-mystic undertones, does it matter? G K Chesterton (1874-1936) wrote the story of this same battle in his 1911 epic poem, *The*

Ballad of the White Horse. He sets it in the Vale. The battle is won because the Danes, who were professional marauders, slacken too soon and allow Alfred to rally his peasant army, armed with pitchforks and sickles. The Virgin Mary appears to Alfred in a vision the night before the battle. 'Will we win?' he asks her.

> I tell you naught for your comfort,
> Yea, naught for your desire,
> Save that the sky grows darker yet
> And the sea rises higher.

It works as a myth – or a lie which tells a truth, as Dante has it. Imagine a young Victorian on the height above the White Horse looking down over the ripples made by melting ice in the soil of the combe below. A thousand years ago on this same hillside his own people had changed the way the world works. Space, time, and a sphere he can neither grasp nor analyse contracts in his mind to a single timeless point. Something of great importance has happened to him which he can barely put into words and will never therefore ever be able to think clearly about. It's a mystic experience, a glimpse of divinity, on top of undertones which will sustain and enrich him for life.

Hughes was no mystic – he was a lawyer, a Liberal and a Christian Socialist (a strangely confused combination). Chesterton was a mystic, although an unlikely one – he was a twenty stone journalist with a sword stick and a cloak. All the same he had at least one mystical experience, in 1894, when he was at the Slade School of Art. Mysticism he thought was merely common sense. More perceptively he also said: "Every high civilisation decays by forgetting obvious things". If we're reading Hughes correctly, the beginning of that forgetfulness can be traced back at least to the 1850s.

SIX

The Undertones of Patriotism

Kipling is anathema to many people these days, and might be literally so if the people who most revile him were religious. Orwell called him: "an aesthetically disgusting, morally insensitive, coarse, brutal, sadistic, sulky, tawdry, shallow and" – worse? – "*vulgar* gutter patriot." All in a single short review of Eliot's collection of Kipling's verse (as they both called his poetry) in 1942, in the middle of a war.

Rudyard Kipling (1865-1936) was a child of the Raj, albeit a lowly one (his father was an artist and teacher). His early life in England was unhappy and perhaps even brutalised. Later he went to a brash new, and unsuitable, public school – the United Services College at Westward Ho! (the only place ever named after a novel) in Devon. For most of the 1880s he worked as a journalist in India. His wife was American and they lived in Vermont for most of the '90s. In some ways, then, he was a stranger in the world – not an Indian in India, nor an American in America, nor (or not really) an Englishman in England. But he prided himself on being able to 'think in another man's skin'. And even Orwell admitted he was a master story-teller.

Puck of Pook's Hill (1906) and *Rewards and Fairies* (1910) are stories about Puck and two children, a brother and sister called Una and Dan. They're far from average – their father owns the woods and rivers where they play and they're just old enough to be ashamed of having a nursery (they call it the school room). One June they act out their father's version of *A Midsummer Night's Dream* in a fairy ring on the family estate. Unknowingly they summon up Puck, the self same sprite who, in the play, shakes his head over what fools these mortals be. This Puck isn't the usual late Edwardian fairy – he's an Old One, alias Robin Goodfellow, Lob-lie-by-the-fire, or Nick o' Lincoln. He conjures up real people from the past to teach the children their country's history, and create undertones in young readers.

Only *The Knife and the Naked Chalk* is about pre-history. Una and Dan visit a shepherd, Mr Dudeney, on the South Downs which lie between the Wealden hills where they live and the sea. A retired sheepdog guides them to where the old man sits on the rim of a deep hollow where his sheep graze in the heat of August. "Press your face down and smell to the turf," Mr Dudeney tells them. "That's Southdown thyme which makes Southdown mutton beyond compare, and, my mother told me, 'twill cure anything except broken necks, or hearts. I forget which."

They sit in the sun waiting for the shadow of the hills to cool them. Suddenly, Puck and a semi-naked man in a cloak appear to Una and Dan, though not the old shepherd. The man is from the Stone Age. To his tribe he's a god because he gave them magic knives to keep wolves at bay.

Once, when the wolf packs had migrated from the Downs for a while, he drove his sheep close to the forest edge on the High Weald. He didn't dare go in the woods: the Children of the Night were there, and they'd ruin his soul. Then he saw a man of the trees kill a wolf with a knife. What kind of knife? Could he get them for his own people?

Before going into the forest, he told his mother, the priestess, that he was going to deal with the wild men. In the forest, as people said he would, he lost his mind (a fever, Puck hinted). The Children of the Night sweated the madness out of him with steam from water poured over hot rock. When he was cured, he watched them melting red stones (like tallow) and turning them into blades. The magic knives were iron (the redness of the stones was ferrous oxide, or rust). He told the iron people he'd trade mutton, wool and milk for knives. The gods agreed but only if he'd let an eye be gouged out to prove he could be trusted. "What else could I have done?" he asks Puck. "The sheep are the people." What he'd done was right – the iron knives kept the wolves away from his people's children and sheep.

Except, for him, everything has changed. He's now a god,

35

Tyr, whose shadow is too sacred to be stepped on. No one dares touch him. The woman he was to marry left him. He let her go ("What else could I do?). Food and a bed are his for the asking – but not a home of his own, or children.

Now Puck recites "by Oak, Ash and Thorn" to break the spell. Una and Dan forget what's happened. They walk back through the evening shadows of the grass, and the meadow scabious (a flower to cure scabies). Everywhere is the scent of thyme and the sea.

Duty is a theme running through all the Puck stories – but duty also means accepting being treated badly for doing the right thing, which should always be done selflessly. Another theme is continuity. Una, for example, loves the bare short-turfed Downs. "It's just like the sea. You see where you're going, and … you go there and there's nothing between." Mr Dudeney, on the other hand, is in a direct line of descent from Tyr and the flint people of the New Stone Age. He's inherited their distrust of trees, and the tribes of the night who live among them. "There's no profit in trees," he rationalises. "They draw the lightning, and sheep shelter under 'em, and so, like as not, you'll lose a half score ewes struck dead in one storm."

"Trees aren't messy," Una retorts. "And what about firewood? I don't like coal."

You don't get good Southdown thyme in the Weald, the shepherd argues. "Watercress, maybe?"

"But we've water," Una replies. "Brooks full of it – where you can paddle in hot weather."

"Brooks flood. Then you must shift your sheep – let alone foot-rot afterward. I put more dependence on a dewpond any day."

How are dewponds made? Dan asks. He gets no answer – that'd hold up the story – but the question strengthens the point about continuity: this early 20th century shepherd relies on dewponds just as much as his Stone Age kin. Or did they? During those hot Edwardian summers when Kipling was writing *Rewards and Fairies* a geologist called Edward Martin was studying dewponds on the high downland. The geology is porous (it's chalk), there's no artesian source, often they're near the summit seven or eight hundred feet above sea level, and yet they keep their water in droughts when ponds in the valleys are dry. In Sussex they're usually circular, thirty to a hundred feet or so across, never more than four feet deep, and lined with puddled clay. The geologist asked two questions: were dewponds fed by dew, mist, and sea-fog as folklore said, and did the New Stone Age have them? The answers were: no, they relied more on rain and, yes, Neolithic people probably did. Science supported Kipling.

He could get his history mixed up, though. Whoever the Neolithic people were, they weren't Teutons and Tyr is a Germanic god. His English name's Tiw (pronounced tee-oo). From the genitive – Tiwes – we get Tuesday. (It doesn't really matter; a myth is one of the best ways of creating and carrying undertones.) Iron ore, on the other hand, was mined at one time in Sussex: first by the Romans and then again from the Middle Ages to the 18th century. Timber was turned into charcoal to smelt the ore. Wood ran out before the iron, hence the decline.

The writing isn't babyish; death and injustice, for example, are treated matter of factly. Some of the words were unusual even then: 'flinders' was never in common use yet all the same it never needed, or got, a footnote as it does today. Sussex dialect is spoken by the shepherd (sparingly): bivvering for hovering (like a hawk), for example, and baffed for brushed (like summer air on eyelids). Although only thirty miles apart, the accents of the Weald and the Chalk were still very different in the Edwardian era. At that time – and for long after – the county was called Silly Sussex. 'Silly', it was thought, meant 'holy'. (Happy or fortunate is more accurate.) For people who didn't live there (and possibly for some who did) there was something spiritual about the place. Chesterton and Belloc thought so too. (Cornwall had a similar aura, but a Celtic one.)

In all these stories Una and Dan are always made to forget what they've seen. The undertones are reserved for the reader, or the read-to. Kipling the outsider created lifelong undertones – yet another country in the soul – for people now either either dead or old.

SEVEN

A Valley of Vision and the Lonely Tower

Samuel Palmer was born just off the Old Kent Road in South London a few months before the Battle of Trafalgar and died seventy-six years later just before the first oil-driven cars were on the road. (1805-1881, in fact.) His father was a book-seller and sometime Baptist preacher, though his family were quite well-heeled felt makers in the City. Surrey Square, where Samuel was born, was just over ten years old at the time – an incomplete development of Georgian terraced houses with still a fair bit of standing timber. Judging by a self-portrait painted when he was about twenty, Samuel had the kind of Cockney face which was common in south London until fairly recently, except for the sadness in the eyes. He was in fact a mystic for the first forty years of his life.

Was he a classic case of the introvert as mystic? As a boy he had no friends of the same age, played no outdoor games (and only backgammon indoors). Instead he read a lot. In fact he spent his time reading (his father's bookshop was probably very handy). Mary Ward, his nurse saved him from vitamin deficiency at the hands of his unskilled mother (who died when he was thirteen – he said the pain of it was like being pierced with a sword). His earliest memory was of Mary pointing out the moon shining above the elms in their square. He was four, but whether it was a mystic experience or not doesn't seem to be recorded. (It could have been: Ruskin's first visionary event was at the same age.) Mary also dressed him oddly, even when he was man in his twenties; the coat pockets she made were abnormally large – he could carry two painter's palettes in them as well as books. He also wore an outsized hat and since his legs were short and his body normal, he was a figure of derision to small boys. On her death bed Mary gave him a copy of Milton's shorter poems which he reinforced with brass and carried for twenty years in his waistcoat pocket.

Meanwhile, he only ever had two terms of formal schooling (at Merchant Taylors'). Instead, he had a private drawing master and also went to Flaxman's lectures in the Royal Academy. When he was seventeen he'd already sold one picture and exhibited three others, all under Turner's influence, in the RA's summer hangings. Around this time John Linnell took notice of him and pointed the boy artistically backwards. "Heaven sent him," Palmer later said, "to pluck me from the pit of modern art." Linnell – who later became his father-in-law – also introduced him to Blake, the second great influence on his life (the first was Turner). On one visit, Blake, then an old man, was bed-ridden with a scalded leg but working on his Dante illustrations. The old man told the young one that he began all new work with 'fear and trembling.' "I have enough of that," said Palmer. To which Blake replied: "You'll do."

In particular he was overwhelmed (for a lifetime) by Blake's wood-cuts illustrating Virgil's *Eclogues*. In them (to re-arrange his own words slightly) Palmer saw "the mystic glimmer which penetrates and kindles the inmost soul and gives complete delight unlike the gaudy sunlight of the world."

Palmer is also said to have revered Blake so much that he kissed the old man's door bell (or the threshold, accounts vary) whenever he visited. All the same, Palmer said of himself that he spent most of his time "in stupid apathy, negligence, ignorance, and restless despondency, without any of those delicious visions which are the only joys of my life." But not for long because from the mid-1820s to the mid-30s he lived in a painters' colony in Shoreham in the Darent valley in Kent. What he painted was a pure mystic vision of a kind never done before or since. He called the place the Valley of Vision and the painters called themselves The Ancients, because the old ways were better.

Francis Oliver Finch was a water colour painter and deeply religious. Edward Calvert – a Cornishman and one time Midshipman – was one of the 19th century's great engravers. Frederick Tatham was a sculptor as well as a painter. For a time he and Palmer shared Rat Abbey, the cottage which Palmer bought out of his own small private income. John Giles was Palmer's cousin. Henry Walter was a water colourist. Welby Sherman was another engraver: he welshed on a gambling debt – billiards, apparently – owed to Palmer's brother and decamped overseas. There was also George Richmond, a life long friend, who grew rich later in the century by painting portraits of the fashionable. Palmer's father turned up as well, having been bribed by his rich felt-making brother to give up book selling in order to live like a gentleman. His house was the overspill dormitory for Samuel's visitors when Rat Abbey was full. (Mary Ward went along as well.)

The locals mistook The Ancients for star gazing astrologers and called them 'extollagers'. The 1830s was a time of social unrest – the decade of the Swing riots and Tolpuddle Martyrs. Rioters broke threshing machines, set fire to hay ricks, and burned down tithe barns (who Captain Swing was, if anybody, nobody knows). (Palmer wasn't entirely oblivious of all this: in 1832 he wrote a pamphlet – condemning the rioters.) All the same, he went on painting mysticism, mainly in the shape of moonlight on a deeply rural landscape and richly blossomed orchards and corn fields. In a letter to Richmond he said he'd put up with anything so long as he could sometimes "look over the doors of bliss". And of course he did, all mystics do, even lesser ones. Could he, however, open the way for others to peer over the doors as well?

He was twenty-five when he painted *Coming from Evening Church*. The medium is oil and tempera (in this case, carpenter's glue) and the picture hasn't worn too well. At first it looks like old sun-bubbled paint or tar on a gate post or garden fence, a dark, knobbly picture with unlikely green hills about to fall over on to a church and its congregation as they walk home in a long crocodile under a Harvest moon. The lead figures are a husband and wife. She's tall and slender, in a straw sun bonnet and a red dress belted just below the bosom. Her face is very strange. Is she stunned with grief, exalted, or just badly painted? Her husband has a red beard and dark clothes. They're passing the garden gate of a cottage with a lattice window. Their son is in a velvet green suit. Grandparents walk behind – he with a white Biblical beard and white clothes. Apart from two small children, a woman holding a baby, and an old man with a ragged staff and beard, the rest of the column have few features, wrapped as they are in cloaks or shawls like Petruschka dolls. The priest stands alone in a loop of the crocodile.

For all its dark green and red paint, it's a strangely yellow painting – yellow moon (paint-cracked into mountains and seas), yellow hills and people, and an unnaturally elongated steeple capped with a big stone cross. Life – ivy – climbs the spire. Everything strains upwards – the steeple itself is like a rocket on a launch pad. Its cross is higher than the hills, or the moon. Trees frame it.

It's a strangely silent picture, too – if you could step inside you feel you'd be in a noiseless world. Here is Ruskin's repose at the centre of art. The procession is like a pilgrimage, going not home but Home. Hills like cupped hands lean protectively over. The church, which seems to be cruck-built, is also like cupped hands. Even the sheep on the impossibly leaning hills are penned safely in a tiny square fold.

Palmer's most famous Shoreham picture, also painted when he was twenty-five and called *The Magic Apple Tree*, is an extraordinary combination of curves and colour carrying the eye of the mind through into Stillness: change is arrested to uncover the unchanging which lies below it. Again it's a cupped picture; fully leafed trees arch over a curve of hills which are bright yellow with corn. In the foreground a shepherd plays on a pipe while his flock, like bales of wool, sleep. Through the leaf-arch you see a cone of a church steeple but not this time soaring into the heavens. Instead it's swamped by an apple tree leaning out across the road, every bough laden – impossibly laden – with rich round red apples, an everlasting fecundity of fruit sprouting – or spouting even

– from the timeless eternity you sense (and are drawn into) behind and beyond the paint.

In the foreground of his 1829 painting, *In a Shoreham Garden*, a fruit tree with a sinuous trunk bears great suds of blossom. A path leads the eye to a tranquil lady in a red and white dress with a trailing hem and then carries the mind's eye to tranquillity beyond her. She's too distant to have features but she is looking upwards – at what? Something outside the picture and outside this world? She looks too aetherial for this hard planet and seems to belong elsewhere.

In 1835 with two fellow Ancients, Edward Calvert and Henry Walter, Palmer took a steamer around the coast from London to North Wales. On the way back by road they stopped at Tintern in what was then Monmouthshire. There he made a very beautiful study of a house and garden in pen and ink, gouache (or body colour as art historians call it), watercolour and black chalk. At first glance it looks like a self-coloured wash of attractive rusty-brown-beige with a sketched-in house and garden. Then you notice the very detailed fig tree with a spot of yellow. Some roof tiles are also detailed. The windows are just black marks but the sky is slightly pink. In front of the fig tree are tall, sketched-in hollyhocks. To the left is the winter-like outline of the bare spreading boughs of a tree; bare, that is, until you notice that foliage is suggested by the vaguest and most lightly coloured haze of creamy-beige. Cobblestones fill the foreground. For those so inclined it's a window-picture through which you can see Profundity beyond (or, rather, it slows thought allowing the Beyond to well up and take everyday reality's place). A combination of the finished and the sketchy became a bit of a Palmer hallmark. It works, semi-mystically, very well. Perhaps the mind doesn't get so bogged down in detail and therefore better able to semi-shut-down. (Tintern figures, as we'll see, in the works of two other mystics – Wordsworth ad Tennyson.)

42

He painted half a dozen waterfalls in Wales. One, *Pistyll Mawddach*, is framed by crags and great trees (again that feeling of cupped hands sheltering and holding nature). The water itself pours abruptly into the landscape in the top quarter of the picture. He hasn't caught the falling water with Turner's skill in Teesdale but it's better in a different way: change has here been arrested and turned into a vision of something changeless. In another picture, *The Black Waterfall, near Dolgelly* (in fact Dolgellau), the water falls in two stages through a ravine cupped by delicate birch trees. There's an unworldly or other-worldly blueness about the picture: the water is blue-tinged and some of the rocks and the bark of the silver birches are blue. The eye however doesn't fall with the river: it rises to a gap in the trees, then into whatever is beyond.

In June, 1836, he was again in Wales and wrote: "Blessed thoughts and visions haunt the Stillness and the twilight of the Soul; and one of the great arts of life is the manufacturing of this stillness." He might have added that one of the great arts of art is to close the minds and open the eyes of other people so that they, too, can reach through to Stillness. He does so in both early and late work, but more luminously in the earlier.

Palmer married Linnell's daughter, Hannah, in 1837. She was fifteen years younger. They began married life with a two year working honeymoon in Italy (even Hannah was commissioned to do some drawings for her father). Oddly enough they travelled with George Richmond and his family. Years later Palmer's son said Richmond had been "suave, courtly, dictatorial" while Palmer was "short, shabby (but handsome) with his strange big-pocketed coat and habit of cracking nuts with his teeth." What happened next was a pointer to Palmer's life to be. Richmond mixed with society and made money. Palmer didn't. Back in England, Linnell made a fortune, while the Palmers often relied on him for help. In London most of Palmer's earned income was from teaching.

Introversion could explain some of the things about him – a blindness to reality, to begin with. People like him can be stubborn yet suddenly buckle, even grovel, when faced by stronger personalities. There was something of this in

43

Palmer's dealings with his father-in-law, an over-bearing and sneering character. Linnell was also a fundamentalist who was down on priests (he flirted with – but never joined – both the Quakers and the Plymouth Brethren). Because of his beliefs, he seems to have forced Palmer to marry in a registrar's office, something Palmer was uneasy about for the rest of his life (he was very devout Anglican). Yet Palmer was thirty-two at the time, on the verge of middle age, and Linnell was still only forty-five.

At times there was a hint of abasement. "I am very much obliged," he wrote to Linnell, " by your careful and excellent advice which I will attend to, and endeavour to follow: and I hope from time to time you will communicate any suggestions that arise in your mind – as I am out of the way of instruction and left to my own resources."

On top of all that he was a snuff-taking asthmatic reactionary creationist. His later work isn't as idiosyncratic as it was in his mystic heyday but it wasn't Victorian enough for the Victorians, either. (*Tintagel Castle, Approaching Rain* (1848) is outstanding but not something many Victorians would have bought: it centres on a great swirl of gold and sand-coloured rock into which the castle has settled with age. The Romanesque doorway is like an entrance to a cave. Gulls fly under the stone by the sea.)

As a young man, Linnell had also had an original eye – his trees, buildings, and barges look modern even today. Yet the work which bought him seventy acres of Surrey was fully Victorian – shepherdesses in an English Arcadia and flocks and herds wending home to fold and byre, as well as more down to earth pictures of, for example, sand and gravel pits on Hampstead Heath and in Kensington. (George Richmond thought Linnell may have owed more to Palmer than the other way around.)

Palmer was nearly fifty before he became a full member of the Watercolour Society and could show his work in public. Even Ruskin saw little in him; of Palmer's *Going to India* (1858) he said 'looks at first cruder and harsher than it is, but gains by a long look, and has deep feeling in it'. After his death, Palmer largely dropped out of sight until the V&A held an exhibition of a few of his pictures in 1926. In 1909 Palmer's son, Alfred Herbert Palmer had burned a lot of the early work and notebooks – the bonfire had burned for two days, it's said. All the same Palmer was one of the influences on the Brotherhood of Ruralists in the 1970s and the Neo-Romantics (at least one of whom, John Piper, was a minor mystic) between the Wars.

The Palmers' daughter, Mary Elizabeth, died, aged three, in 1844. Their oldest son, Thomas More Palmer, died aged nineteen in 1861 of scarlet fever, leaving his father distraught: he'd set high hopes on the boy and may have driven him too hard, drumming religion into him in ways that perhaps weren't too healthy. Palmer now called the earth a 'den of horrors'. Out of all this unhappiness came the largest picture he ever did – just over two feet by nearly three and half: *A Dream in the Apennines* (1864), painted perhaps to drive out the pain. "My earthly hopes are in the grave," he wrote, referring to the death of his son." He added: "When men are happy they seldom know it." People snatch at the shadows of happiness and miss the real thing.

A Dream in the Apennines is a standard painting of Italian light and landscape, albeit from memory and sketches made long ago when he was young. In the foreground, a man with an ox cart is about to drive away as a child loads the last of the grapes. A young woman leans on a low wall above a ravine and a river. There are goats, and a great sweep of red-streaked sky and the plains stretching away to an unseen sea. To Ruskin's question – "does it make people bigger and better?" – the answer is, yes, if only slightly. You get no sense of God walking in the cool of the evening. However you do get undertones of day's ending, *all* days' endings.

There was a happy ending, though. In his old age he broke with Linnell and grew closer to his wife again: they went to church together and took drives in the country. In his last few years they lived first in Reigate and then Redhill where Palmer had his own small studio, barred to all but himself, with a patch of soil for his own wild flowers. The rest of the house and garden, Mrs Palmer's domain, were tidy, dust-free and regimented.

He'd also begun a new career, as an etcher. Some etchings were for his own translation of Virgil's *Eclogues*, others were commissioned by Ruskin's solicitor, a man called Leonard Valpy (who paid little and wanted to pay less) to illustrate Milton's *L'Allegro* and *Il Penseroso*. Not many were finished.

The preliminary picture, *Opening the Fold*, which he made for a Virgil etching (and never made) is very beautiful, and clearly in a line with his Shoreham days. It's a brown wash. A shepherd leans, piping, against a slender tree while his flock (too densely packed in reality for grazing) graze in the foreground. A tall slender tree with a high thin canopy stands at the head of a shallow valley running down to the plains. The thatched roof of a cottage, with a smoke rising from the chimney, appears unobtrusively on the right in a glade of its own. Then the eye is carried up to strange mountains, eroded into shapes like carious teeth, on the horizon, and then beyond them to the deeper Beyond. The touch of the old mysticism is here but toned down by time, an afterglow that for some is even more effective than the old exuberance.

The Lonely Tower illustrates a passage in *Il Penseroso*:

> Or let my lamp at midnight hour
> Be seen in some high lonely tower
> Where I may oft outwatch the Bear
> With thrice-great Hermes, or unsphere
> The spirit of Plato to unfold
> What worlds or what vast regions hold
> The immortal mind that hath forsook
> Her mansion in this fleshly nook.

Aristotle distinguished between black and golden melancholy (Burton does something similar in *The Anatomy of Melancholy*); this poem is about the golden kind which can lead un penseroso, or thoughtful man, to mystic union with the divine. (As we'll see, a mood of sadness for the loneliness of things is usually essential to mystic poetry.) 'Thrice great Hermes' is not the messenger of the gods but the sage who wrote about mysticism in the early Christian era. (He was surnamed Trismegistus – thrice great.) Plato, of course, believed an immortal world exists beyond the fleshly nook of the body and its limited senses. 'To outwatch the Bear' means to stay up all night, since the constellation of the Great Bear or Plough and the Pole Star never set. Plato would have agreed that night-long reading could bring about the mystic experience – if (as we know today) in ends in mental shut-down.

There's a light in Palmer's tower and a big sickle moon lying on her back on the far horizon. It lights (brilliantly) part of the sky, and streaks of cloud, and then shines on a flock of sheep and two shepherds. It also shines on the trunks of a clump of trees whose foliage leans over and, in turn, seem to shade the moon, just like the cupped hand landscapes of his younger days. A wagon toils up the shaded side of the hill. The etching catches the mystery of mysticism, and is certainly a strong undercurrent or undertone even if not a complete mind-stopper.

Some say the tower in Palmer's etching was modelled on one near Lynmouth in Devon. On the other hand, there was (still is) a not dissimilar tower on the top of Leith Hill in Surrey which may well have been the model for the rising ground in the picture. (Palmer's son had died near there and his own studio was nearby.) The Surrey Hills in those days were denuded of trees (unlike today) just as they are in the etching. There are no gorges in the hills as there is in the foreground, but even that might be an illusion since it's too dark to see. In an 1868 watercolour of the same scene the bottom of the 'gorge' is visible and it's not too deeply impossible for the Surrey Hills, scored as they are by gills flowing in mini-ravines

Palmer was then an old man of seventy-three. His great mystic period had lasted for ten years, half a century ago: this was his lesser mystic swan song. As he etched his copper plates in his studio, another minor mystic – the seven year old Ralph Vaughan Williams – was growing up in the big house on the lower slopes of Leith Hill just below the lonely tower.

EIGHT

Music and the Common Mystic

Ralph Vaughan Williams (1872-1958) was a lifelong mystic although of the lesser kind in all probability. As early as 1903, when he was twenty one, he quoted Carlyle: "If we search deep enough there is music everywhere." In 1920, when he was forty-eight, he said art exists to reveal the spiritual to which the senses are blind. In 1932, aged sixty, he said: "The object of art is to stretch out to the ultimate realities through the medium of beauty". Music, he said in 1942, when he was seventy, was a 'spiritual experience'. After the War, people would have to turn back to the eternal. (They never did.) Even in his eighties he could fall into a silence bordering on trance over the beauty of a sunset. In 1958, aged eighty-six, he wrote to the children in a primary school in Swaffham in Norfolk. Music, he told them, lets you see the essence of things in a way science can't: the arts open 'magic casements' through which to see what lies beyond.

Vaughan Williams was born in Gloucestershire in 1872 but taken to Leith Hill Place, his mother's old home, when he was three. Leith Hill, just short of a thousand feet, is the highest point in Surrey (the southern kingdom in the speech of the South Saxons). The tower on the crest – an 18th century folly – may have been the model for Palmer's etching for Milton's *Il Penseroso*; it's roughly the same shape. It also raises the hills to just over a thousand feet which was once the definition of a mountain.

Leith Hill Place is on the lower slopes of the hills but high enough to have a view across the Low Weald to the South Downs. The Low Weald is so well wooded it looks like a forest and the Downs are distant enough to be blue. King

Alfred the Great's father, Ethelwulf, defeated the Danes here in 851. A mass grave, possibly of men who died there, was unearthed when young Ralph was ten years old.

For a mystically inclined child it must have been more like a portal than a place, opening on to that ultimate reality he spoke about. Childhood should have been perfect – kindness and culture, money and space (the walled kitchen garden across the lane from the big house is four acres on its own). The family woods had been inter-planted with azaleas and rhododendrons. Old stone pits had returned to nature as ponds, some big enough for swimming in. When he was older he had an organ in the hall where he practised before breakfast. Working the bellows was the problem. The butler had to lay the table. A groom or gardener was corralled occasionally. More usually it was one of the maids who was then put behind with her work.

Not a lot of science was taught but at least Great-Uncle Charles, who tipped half a crown when he visited, was the author of *The Origins of Species*. (As girls, Vaughan Williams's mother and aunt were asked to do research for him. Are the stalks of the bird's nest orchis, for example, straight or curved when they first sprout?)

Vaughan Williams went first to Charterhouse, then the Royal College of Music (under Parry), then Cambridge (in 1892), then back to the RCM where he studied under Stanford and made a life long friend of Holst, a fellow mystic who was influenced by Hinduism. In 1897 he studied under Max Bruch in Berlin. (Much later Ravel taught him orchestration in Paris.)

In 1914 although, at forty-one, old enough to avoid war service he enlisted as a private in the RAMC and served with an ambulance unit on the Western Front. *A Pastoral Symphony* was conceived at this time. People thought it was a threnody for the long, lost, summers of Edwardian England. He said otherwise: "It's really war-time music, a great deal of it incubated when I used to go up night after night with the ambulance waggon at Ecoivres and we went up a steep hill and there was a wonderful Corot-like landscape in the sunset – and it's not really lambkins at all as most people take for granted." Then he was posted to Salonika before returning to the Front as a lieutenant in the Royal Garrison Artillery and into action with their heavy guns in the last months of the War. After the Armistice, still in uniform, he became the First Army's Director of Music, organising orchestras and choirs among troops now waiting to be demobbed.

He married twice. Adeline Fisher, his first wife, was a cousin of Virginia Woolf. His second, Ursula, was forty years his junior. She was the daughter of a Major-General and widow of a half Colonel. For twenty years Vaughan Williams was professor of composition in the RCM. But also a writer, broadcaster, lecturer, conductor and, of course, composer. By the time he died in 1958, aged eighty-six, he'd written close to five hundred individual pieces of music, including operas, oratorios, church and chamber music, concertos (one for the mouth organ), songs, hymns, ballet and choral music, incidental music for the theatre and radio, marches, film scores, and nine symphonies, the last in his last year of life. The night he died, in his sleep, he was still working, planning a future.

What exactly he experienced, mystically, doesn't seem to be known but it was music, as you'd expect, which was the trigger – music and possibly landscape and love of country. This wasn't unusual. What a mystic sees is a singleness below all created things which gives a feeling of belonging to something greater than the self. Unsurprisingly, then, Vaughan Williams thought folk music was the embodiment of a country's deepest being. All great art is rooted in a sense of belonging to a country with a continuity of language, history, art, law, philosophy, customs and shared memories. More than that, without these things there can be no art at all. "A colourless cosmopolitanism may produce a crowd of dilettante gourmets, but it will never produce a creative artist." Art can be global only if it's local to begin with: you can't create a garden where wild flowers won't grow. This wasn't jingoism, he insisted. Still less was it nationalism, or even patriotism: it was a fact of life.

For the same reason he composed sacred music and compiled the *English Hymnal* even though he was an agnostic, albeit one who'd upgraded from atheist. ("There is no reason why an atheist could not write a good Mass.") He was also an historian (he'd read history in Cambridge) awake to continuity; if a national culture is needed then, in England, Christianity has to be part of it. Only once, in fact, did England have a school of composers and that was when three things came together: Reformation religion, Renaissance secularism, and a closeness between high-brow and middle-brow music. The Tudor school of composers (Byrd, Tallis, Willbye, Weelkes, Farrant, Morley, Dowland, Gibbons) wrote both church music and secular madrigals, anthems and choral works, along with pieces for the virginals and lute to be played at home.

They could do so because all levels of music shared the same root and could cross-fertilise each other. After Purcell, they went separate ways – the high-brow going Continental while the low retreated to the country, only occasionally breaking through as city ballads or *The Beggar's Opera*. The folk singing tradition began to wind down after 1860 (or so he thought) because by then the railways had had time to carry London ways to remote places. By the 1900s the singers were mostly in their seventies or older.

In the early 20th century he gave a series of lectures on folk music. Astonishingly, in a country where folk songs were still sung without affectation in village ale houses, he lectured from a book. Worse, the material had been collected sixty years earlier by a man who had also lived, in a strange twist of coincidence, on Leith Hill. In 1903 Vaughan Williams was lecturing in Essex. Two ladies in his audience asked him if he'd like to meet a real folk singer in their own village of Ingrave. Through them he met an old shepherd called Charles Pottipher who sang *Bushes and Briars* for him. After that, he began collecting for himself. He also began using folk music in his own work. *In the Fen Country* dates from this time (1904), a *Norfolk Rhapsody* from two year later. Both are based on folk songs he'd collected – in particular from King's

Lynn where the Viking-descended fishermen still lived apart from the rest of the town.

But is his music right for the common mystic? Music can't be called mystical if it doesn't evoke Eternity in the listener; what the composer intended doesn't matter. Vaughan Williams was an admirer of Walt Whitman, a fellow mystic, whose verses about the quest for spiritual insight he'd already set to music in his pre-Great War *Sea Symphony*. In it the mystic vision is explicitly laid out – all things are interwoven because all things are ultimately made of the same thing, or non-thing; it's an interlacing of sameness, not difference. *Sancta Civitas* (The Holy City), written in the early 1920s, was his own favourite choral work. It's short – around half an hour – and dense with sound, packed with intellectual meaning. It's often said to be mystical, though what people mean by that is never explained. His second wife said it summed up his beliefs – 'all will be well', the timeless message of the mystic.

Neither piece – however good or great they may be – works mystically, or in raising undertones. He was addicted to loud passages in quiet pieces, and just loud pieces. (In places *Sancta Civitas* is played *triple forte* by the brass.) A reasonable rule of thumb says that loud, raucous, brassy music is unmystical, incapable of invoking essential serenity and a mood of sadness. (The problem is blaring brassiness; many Tudor and later pieces for valveless trumpets do work minor mystically.)

The mistake seems to be in thinking that describing the mystic vision *is* the mystic vision. It isn't for the simple reason that it's indescribable. It can only be experienced. Descriptive art can do that – possibly even this oratorio can for some people – but it's unlikely. If mysticism is about concord it's hard to see how discord can reach it; and a lot of his music is discordant.

Of his nine symphonies, only two – the *Pastoral* and the Fifth – are close to what is needed. The problem with them seems to be bittiness. Something sad and sweeping is needed, not subtle bits talking cleverly to each to other. *The Pastoral*

Symphony starts off well but soon falls into this musical chatter. The same strictures apply to his other quiet symphony, the Fifth, played for the first time in 1943. If audiences thought the *Pastoral* was looking back to peace-before-war, they thought the Fifth looked ahead to peace-after-it. Unfortunately it'd been written in 1938, a fact which didn't seem to end people's belief.

Was he, then, just too cerebral? Mistakenly he did think that the intellect is the cause of what he called the 'mystic outlook'. Holst, he said, had reached his mysticism 'through deep thought'. Yet no-thought, not deep thought, is the way in. Whatever stops thinking wins.

Mysticism, he also thought, can be expressed through melisma, and (apparently) he consciously wrote it. (In the 1936 Hollywood musical, *Rose Marie*, Nelson Eddy and Jeanette MacDonald sing a duet with the line: "When I'm calling you Oo-Oo-Oo-Oo-Oo-Oo-Oo-Oo." Oo-Oo-Oo-etc. is melismatic – running a single syllable up and down a scale.) Cantors and gospel singers use it, as does Plainsong. But a church has an advantage over a concert hall – everything is designed to evoke the eternal. To step into an Orthodox cathedral is to step out of time into Eternity, helped by melismatic Byzantine chant and a long drawn out ison, or bass drone.

On the other hand, Vaughan Williams did write some music for common mystics and, not surprisingly (unsurprising, that is, if millions of people are open to the spiritual) it's also the stock in trade of the popular classical radio stations: *The Lark Ascending*, *Fantasia on Greensleeves*, and most especially *The Fantasia on a Theme of Thomas Tallis* is one of the greatest works for the minor mystic in all English music. (Whether it's a great work in its own right is neither here nor there.)

Two of these tunes are Tudor (fantasia means variations on somebody else's work). His *Greensleeves* is pretty much the unadorned and unaltered 16th century tune. The adaptation began as incidental music for *The Merry Wives of Windsor* in 1912. (Falstaff says: "Let the sky rain potatoes, let it thunder to the tune of *Greensleeves*".) In its own day, *Greensleeves* was a hymn, a dance tune, and the lament of a man deserted by his lover who, possibly, is also a prostitute (green carried that meaning). The spiritual and the earthy (let alone earthly) were fused. The traditional words are also simple and moving, catching exactly the needed feeling of sadness that lies at the heart of life, and the loneliness of things:

> Alas, my love, you do me wrong
> To cast me off discourteously
> For I have loved you well and long,
> Delighting in your company.
>
> Greensleeves was all my joy,
> Greensleeves was my delight,
> Greensleeves was my heart of gold,
> And who but my Lady Greensleeves?

The Lark Ascending seems strangely modern in a 21st century when nobody could possibly write anything like it. Perhaps, therefore, it's timeless? It was certainly unfashionable when it was first performed in 1920 – the era of Edith Sitwell's *Façade* and the Bright Young Things. In fact Vaughan Williams started to write it pre-Great War for the violinist Marie Hall. It accurately turns into music the words of a poem by another Victorian mystic, George Meredith. The poem is a short-long one, a hundred and twenty odd lines, matched almost exactly by the music at around fifteen minutes. In *An Oxford Elegy* (his setting of Arnold's *The Scholar Gipsy*) the music is inferior to the poetry: here it's superior. The lark

> ... rises and begins to round,
> He drops the silver chain of sound,
> Of many links without a break,
> In chirrup, whistle, slur and shake.
>
> For singing 'til his heaven fills,
> 'Tis love of earth that he instils,
> And ever winging up and up,
> Our valley is his golden cup,

And he the wine which overflows
To lift us with him as he goes:
The woods and brooks, the sheep and kine
He is, the hills, the human line,
The meadows green, the fallow brown.

What is missing from *An Oxford Elegy* is all here: a pastoral portrayal. The valley like a golden cup could be a dip in the Cumnor Hills filled with ripening wheat. (The composer probably had the high chalk plains of Wiltshire in mind.) Even the last line is caught and turned into a cadenza. Musicologists may not say much about it – what is there to say? – but it's a favourite of the radio programmes, again possibly because of its lesser mysticism inducing quality.

The right melody will speak directly to the hearing mind (let alone the listening one) and you get it in full in the *Tallis* suite which was written to be performed in Gloucester Cathedral as part of the 1910 Three Choirs Festival. Vaughan Williams had been asked to write it, so it was composed with the acoustics of a medieval cathedral in mind. It's based on a hymn written in the Phrygian mode by Thomas Tallis, the organist and composer, for the Archbishop of Canterbury's 1567 *Psalter*. It was composed for religion and then re-composed for a religious place by an atheist with mystic leanings.

Holst is said to have walked the streets of the city all night in a daze after hearing it. Not everybody was so enchanted, but the critic from *The Times* wrote: "Throughout its course one is never quite sure whether one is listening to something very old or very new." He was listening to both (and it's now a century old itself) but perhaps he meant it was out of time and therefore timeless. It's short, fifteen to twenty minutes at the extremes – it isn't music for concentrating on; more for being carried through the magic casement by.

Music is the best and easiest way to gain a minor mystic experience: a few bars of it can often shut down thinking immediately. Not all music, of course, though perhaps all types or genres. The beat of pop music can be like a mantra.

Loud music – any noise – above eighty or ninety decibels (high enough, that is, to start deafening the hearer) will stop thought, though whether it just stuns the brain (rather like a blow to the head) is another matter – perhaps that's part of the appeal of rock music? Melody and harmony in classical music seems to be what stops thought, particularly in slow movements expressing sadness.

NINE

Kado: the Way of Words

"Does this make us bigger and better?" is the only question people need ask – or so said Ruskin – and it applies to everything, politics and art in particular. The idea's a distant echo of Aristotle who thought life's about growth – physical, moral, intellectual, spiritual. The end of human life, he thought, is entelechy – a state of being when all that was potential inside you has been made actual. The result is fulfilment or eudemony, a life lived well and successfully – joyously, too, if joy is a by-product of obeying the nature of things. For many people – a sizeable minority, at least – spirituality is in the genes; eudemony, therefore, is impossible without it.

Art is there to help in all this – either by shutting down the mind and inducing a mild mystic experience or through undertones. Not all art can work this way (some is negative and diminishes people). Most art, in fact, gets nowhere near inducing a mystic moment although it can create undertones. The Hornblower novels are adventure yarns which can give people two things. Facts, to begin with, about the sailing navy – how ships and guns were worked, what life was like in a man o' war, the names of nautical things (orlop, deadeyes, mizzen top, bilboes). They can also dispense undertones – or Masefield's fragments – to make the mind grow, if only by adding a dimension about a way of life which otherwise would be unknowable.

Children's books are particularly good at this – creating undertones is what they're for, after all. Boys who read (or read in the past) *Treasure Island* also take in lifelong undertones revolving around Long John Silver, Blind Pew, Billy Bones, Captain Flint calling for rum as he lies dying in Savannah. Or Ben Gunn craving a little bit of Christian toasted cheese – not that he said that exactly, of course, no more than Holmes said 'elementary, my dear Watson': the undertones of a myth often improve the original.

Kenneth Grahame's *The Wind in the Willows* (1908) works more gently, what with messing about in boats on a sunlit river, or having supper in Badger's many-chambered lair, or Toad careering along Edwardian highways in open topped cars. There's also a description of what seems to be a genuine mystic moment when Mole and Ratty go looking for the lost baby otter and meet the Piper at the Gates of Dawn. "This is the place of my song-dream, the place the music played to me," whispered the Rat, as if in a trance. "Here, in this holy place, here if anywhere surely we shall find Him!" And of course they do but, being small furry animals, their god is goat-hoofed Pan. Was Grahame (1859-1932) another Victorian minor mystic (the century was full of them)?

The Wind in the Willows was turned into a stage play by A A Milne (1882-1956) as *Toad of Toad Hall* – without the Gates of Dawn episode. Milne's own books about Winnie the Pooh are gentler still. There's even a book – *The Tao of Pooh* by Benjamin Hoff – which argues that the honey-loving bear of little brain, exemplifies Taoism, the Chinese mystical philosophy of obedience to the inner nature of things ('go with the flow' in summary). The Tao or Way is the simplicity underlying the material world, or the Unlimited below the Limited, the mystic's unity under diversity. To experience it, you drop all thought: to learn, you add. The book, on the other hand, glorifies ignorance – ignoring the fact that to obey its own inner nature the mind needs knowledge. Pooh and Piglet, Eeyore and Roo, are best read as a childhood undertones. Undertones are a way to the Way, as well.

Poetry is more intense and so can be more intensely mystical. It consists, of course, of form and content – or what's said and the way that it's said; noise plus images, or a kind of music and a kind of painting. Poetry can therefore stop the mind in either of two ways; through sight or through sound – through sound when there's a euphony of syllables strung in a line like musical notes; through sight when images are carried into the mind.

Japanese haiku is the end point, the peak, the highest development of the sight kind of poetry. Because they're so concrete, they work very well in English prose in spite of poetry always getting lost in translation. All the haiku here are the prose translations, freely doctored, of R H Blyth who compiled six volumes of them: *Haiku* (4 vols, 1940s) and *A History of Haiku* (2 vols, 1960s). Blyth was a bit of misfit, a disaffected Englishman of quite a common kind – Orwell had a lot to say about people like him: normally, until the fall of the Berlin Wall, they transferred their loyalty to the Soviet Union and Communism. Blyth was unusual only in transferring his to Zen and the Mikado – in the middle of the Second World War. He was a conscientious objector in World War I and tried to take out Japanese citizenship in World War II. If the Japanese had let him, he might – given the strength of feeling in those days – have been hanged for treason. As it was he lived long enough to help draft the Mikado's denial of divinity and to teach English to the Crown Prince. Blyth, who was born in Essex in 1898 (his father was a railway clerk), studied English in London University and left England for good in 1925. He seems to have read nothing later than that, although he was a professor of English Literature in Japan where he died in 1964.

What is Zen? Among many less coherent things, Blyth says Zen is Love, love of what-really-is, love of the cosmos of which you are an uncreated, inseparable part. Not *in* it, but *of* it. Not made, but (like all things) pure unalloyed Being without moving parts. Zen *roshi* – men and women who've achieved enlightenment – are professional, voluntary mystics who've worked hard for their mystic experiences whereas in the West mysticism has usually been accidental and involuntary. In Zen the mystic moment is called satori – awakening or enlightenment. Without it things have no meaning and all is joyless and pain filled. Negatively, satori grants you freedom from mean-spirited thoughts which diminish and destroy you. Positively, it gives meaning, an acceptance of the inevitable and freedom from too much pain. It comes in different degrees but at the top of the range it answers the question: "What's it all about, Alfie?"

Zen has many routes to enlightenment including *kado* – the way (*do*) of the poet (*ka*) or, more specifically, the way of the writer of haiku. Haiku, it can be argued, were designed to bring about smaller revelations, or minor *satori*. (Some argue that Blyth's link between haiku and Zen was overdone. To an outsider they certainly appear connected.)

Brevity is built in to haiku. The Japanese *haijin*, or haiku poet, has only seventeen syllables (or *onji*) to work with, and at least one of those – in the old days – was a season word, while another indicated a pause. Originally haiku were called hokku which was (still is) the opening verse of a long poem jointly written by different people. Haiku evolved as a free-standing stanza in the late 17th century, mainly through Bashō (1644-1698), who was (possibly) a samurai by birth, a wandering poet and teacher by choice or necessity. Bashō, his pen name, means banana plant. To write haiku he said you need mystery, tranquillity, simplicity, elegance and grace – they very things they uncover and reveal. Furthermore, haiku are found, not made – clear the mind, bow to ultimate reality, breathe out the false, breathe in the Buddha-nature, and let the cosmos compose the poem for you. Because they're sacraments, says Blyth, they don't have meaning, they *are* meaning because they open the door in the wall to let Eternity through.

Why they work is not really known. How they work, on the other hand, is: an image of something manmade is struck against something natural: "umbrellas in a ferry in rain on a river," for example. They are ways to salvation through the sadness of beauty, not a reflection of (or on) the world's badness. A mood of sadness is also therefore essential. A *haijin* can detect four moods. English has no word for them collectively, let alone individually. The best it can do is 'tears for things', taken from the Latin *lachrymae rerum*. Japanese (according to Blyth) has *aware* (sadness at the fleetingness of things), *sabi* (the loneliness of things), *jugen* (sadness invoked by the mystery at the heart of things) and *wabi* (a sense of greatness.) A quiet sadness is the essence of haiku, as it is of all art which induces spiritual insight. The following are adapted from Blyth's translations.

BASHŌ:
Rain in the tub and the blown banana leaves.

First rain of winter. Alone

Feet on a cool wall. Noon nap.

BUSON:
Evening. The inn roof leaks. A cherry tree droops.

Spring day. Sea rising, falling, all day.

Day darkens on the charcoal seller at the year's end

Young leaves drenched in light from the tower.

Yellow flowers lose their yellowness in lantern light.

Ice in the inkstone in the temple in the hills.

ISSA:
Click-clack. A man in the mist. Who?

The great room is deserted, and still. A day of haze.

OTSUJI:
Spring rain. Between the trees, a path to the sea.

SHIKI:
Summer rain. Alone in the office.

Green shadows of banana leaves on a paper screen.

In the summer heat, white houses by the creek.

Temple gods. Far off, a June sea.

Next door's lamp. Light on the banana leaves.

A lonely railway station. Lotus flowers blooming

(Compare that with Edward Thomas's *Adlestrop* and the deserted country railway station on an afternoon of great heat when "a blackbird sang/Close by, and round him, mistier,/Farther and farther, all the birds/Of Oxfordshire and Gloucestershire".)

Zen and haiku were little known in the West until the occupation of Japan in the mid-1940s. Pre-Great War Imagistes, the avant-garde's first stab at Modernism, thought they were copying haiku, and got it wrong. They tried to write bald descriptions of things but didn't know about striking the natural against the made. T E Hulme, a Pre-Imagiste poet and thinker (killed like so many in the Great War) almost pulled it off:

> Old houses were scaffolding once and workmen
>   whistling

Otherwise, Pound's *In a Station of the Metro* is perhaps their best:

> The apparition of these faces in the crowd;
> Petals on a wet, black bough

Nobody has probably ever been rendered bigger and better by either. All the same, haiku-like lines can be taken from longer poems if they have brevity, are concrete, have a mood of sadness for things, and juxtapose the natural and the man-made. More importantly, these short pieces produce undertones. Many people grow out of Housman, yet some of his lines resonate for life. "In summertime on Bredon," for example, "The bells they sound so clear." And: "On the idle hill of summer". For those old enough, they will also evoke a distant past and a lost country although the mood of sadness for the loneliness of things doesn't depend on memory; it's written into the verse as well.

Writing haiku in English may well be impossible: the language forbids it – all those extra syllables (prepositions, auxiliary verbs and so) perhaps get in the way. All the same English does have haiku-like lines which, as if to prove brevity is essential, are often shortened by mind and memory. Dylan Thomas's *Poem in October* has:

> Pale rain above the dwindling harbour
> And over the sea wet church the size of a snail.

The two syllables of 'over' are two too many. Instinctively we shorten it to: "Pale rain over the dwindling harbour. And the sea wet church, the size of a snail".

T S Eliot did something similar:

An old man in a dry month, being read to by a country
    boy, waiting for rain

is not in fact his. It's a tampered-with version of a sentence from E F Benson's biography of Edward Fitzgerald, translator/author of Omar Khayyam. Benson wrote: "Here he sits, in a dry month, old and blind, being read to by a country boy, longing for rain". It works as an undertone if shortened even more: "An old man in a dry month". All three work better if you don't know the context. Fitzgerald in his eccentric old age lived in a farm house near Woodbridge in Suffolk. It says a lot for Victorian village schooling that, when his sight began to go, he hired a local boy to read to him in the evening. Old Fitz sat by the fire in a dressing gown, slippered feet on the fender, snuff box in hand, stroking his beard with a paper-knife, and occasionally mopping his brow with a red silk handkerchief which he kept in the top hat he wore. Knowing all that somehow undermines the undertone, ruins it by switching from the general to a not very appetising and Dickensian particular.

Other haiku-like quotations also work better when the context is unknown. *Recessional*, written in 1897 for the Queen's Diamond Jubilee, is about receding imperial power which Kipling fears will happen, since all things end. Most people shy away from Kipling nowadays. But, taken out of context, one couplet lives on as a timeless undertone in its own right:

The tumult and the shouting dies,
The captains and the kings depart.

Why does it work? Perhaps because it can stand alone without a back story but with a sadness for the passing of any unnamed, unknown things to give it a universality. It captures a sadness of the fleetingness, the passing-ness of *all* things,

Other undertone-producing lines, on the other hand, do benefit if their background is known. For example Wordsworth's

> For old, unhappy, far-off things,
> And battles long ago.

A young woman is singing in Gaelic as she reaps corn alone in a field in the Highlands. What is the song about? Who knows? Old, unhappy, far-off things and battles long ago? It adds to the sadness already there – sadness for things, for the passing of things, the mystery of things.

Sailing to Byzantium is different again. It's so obscure it's usually read with a crib, although none of the crib-writers explain the hard bits. Yeats (1865-1939) wrote it in his early sixties, hardly aged these days, but it can be taken as an old man's thoughts turning to Eternity and away from the swarming sensual life of earth, so busy with getting, begetting, and dying that monuments to unageing intellect are neglected. If he could have spent one month in Antiquity, he wrote, Byzantium would have been the place. "I think I could find in some little wine-shop some philosophical worker in mosaic who would answer all my questions, the supernatural descending nearer to him than to Plotinus even." He saw it as city of narrow streets filled with wine-shops, goldsmiths, and workers in enamel, where heaven was close to earth. Knowing all this adds yet more undertones to:

> And therefore I have sailed the seas and come
> To the holy city of Byzantium.

Need the words make sense? On the whole, yes, if only because, when confronted with a puzzle, the mind won't rest until it's solved. Two quotations from Shakespeare illustrate the point: "Time, hath, my lord, a wallet at his back wherein he puts alms for oblivion" is clearly pure poetry but what does it mean? Fretting away at it stops any mental shut down at all and renders it practically useless as an undertone. "Finish, good lady, the bright day is done, and we are for the dark" has an obvious meaning, an unobvious undertone-meaning, and

64

is a line good enough to stop conscious thought in its own right. As pure sound it's not as good as 'alms for oblivion' but it works better sub- or semi-mystically.

Obscure lines can work when the meaning becomes known and the riddle's solved. They then go on working even if the meaning is lost again. For example:

> Time held me green and dying
> Though I sang in my chains like the sea.

Dylan Thomas is stating the obvious: however young or green we are, we're all decaying and going to die. Like Shakespeare's "the bright day is done" it has an added resonance because it's a truth we all know. Meaning here reinforces the power of sound.

Occasionally, as is the way with most things, none of the above apply. Some lines work even when the meaning is slippery;

> Vacant shuttles weave the wind

conveys cosmic desolation though the meaning is never really clear and won't stand too much probing. It's memorable and can be quoted out of context which, since the context is Eliot's *Gerontion* (a difficult piece), is just as well.

With yet others, the meaning, though known, is scarcely worth bothering with. They still work.

> I am the Mower, Damon, known
> Through all the meadows I have mown.

Marvell seemed strangely taken up by mowing meadows. He turned haymaking into undertones, once read (or heard) never forgotten. Was the Member of Parliament for Hull a closet mystic?

The simplest test of true poetry is memorability. Real poetry is rare. But it's always memorable and memorisable. Does it lodge unasked in the mind and change you? That's what counts. Nothing else. It is then an undertone and therefore spiritual. It might even induce the mystic experience itself. At that level it's *extremely* rare.

65

TEN

Miscellany: Science, Systems, Politics

Science

William Blake (1757-1827) was little known in his life time, and almost completely misunderstood. Time has made up for that (except perhaps for being understood). From time to time there's talk of his poem, *Jerusalem* (as set to music by Hubert Parry) becoming the English national anthem, at least at football matches. A bronze statue of his etching of Sir Isaac Newton squats bent double, wielding callipers, in the forecourt of the British Library. An odd choice, perhaps, given Blake's opinion of science:

> May God us keep?
> From single vision and Newton's sleep.

Compare that with Wordsworth, a fellow mystic, whose bedroom in Cambridge overlooked the chapel where a statue of Newton stood.

> Newton, with his prism and silent face,
> The marble index of a mind for ever
> Voyaging through strange seas of Thought, alone.

Wordsworth's old school, Hawkshead Grammar, taught science (unusually) and Wordsworth was good at maths. Yet he, too, was anti-science:

> One impulse from a vernal wood
> May teach you more of man,
> Of moral evil and of good,
> Than all the sages can.
>
> Sweet is the lore which Nature brings;
> Our meddling intellect

66

Mis-shapes the beauteous forms of things:—
We murder to dissect.

Enough of Science and of Art;
Close up those barren leaves;
Come forth, and bring with you a heartThat watches
    and receives.

Keats also took exception to Natural Philosophy, as science
as still called:

Philosophy will clip an angel's wings,
Conquer all mysteries by rule and line,
Empty the haunted air, and gnomed mine,
Unweave a rainbow.

Looking back you can understand their worries but also
see they were wrong. Science, in the main, is reductionist,
taking things apart to see what makes them tick. Mysticism
deals in wholeness – not just the whole of material life and
matter but also what lies above and below them. The mystic
"watches and receives" as Wordsworth put it. Watching the
woods fretted by a high wind on Wenlock Edge can shut
down thought and induce that vision of inseparable
wholeness. The old poets feared that reducing the same
woods woods to chemicals and cellulose and the hills to rocks
with strange names would get in the way of the vision. It
doesn't, of course;: in fact science can add undertones and
explanations of value to all the lesser breed of mystic.

Knowing for instance that four hundred million years
ago Wenlock Edge was a coral reef in an Ordovician sea
somewhere south of the equator (not far from the present day
Seychelles, apparently) is an amazingly powerful undertone
that will reverberate for a life time. Also the concept of plate
tectonics – how did Shropshire get from the Seychelles to
Shropshire? It sailed there on a plate over the earth's molten
mantle. The hills aren't eternal, but what the mystic sees is (or
so he believes).

Science has evolved since the heyday of the Romantics –
particularly in the last thirty years or so of the 20th century.

Its new theories are of enormous interest to the milder kind of mystic who is never going to see angels hanging like fruit from trees, as Blake did. Complexity Theory, for example, supports Aristotle, Newman, and Arnold who all argued for the well-stocked mind, thinking it necessary to growth and fulfilment. Complexity Theory explains that energy fed into a complex system makes it leap to a higher level of organisation. It works for anything from molecules to city traffic to the well-filled brain. Adding information to the mind, in other words, makes it jump a peg or two closer to the spiritual – the ultimate end of all human activity. If that fails to move you, there's always Systems Theory which says the whole is greater than the sum of the parts.

Chaos Theory is equally useful as an undertone. Complex non-linear systems are inherently unpredictable with order and disorder laid on top of each other. Small changes anywhere in the system can escalate exponentially into great changes in the whole – the Butterfly Effect. Does it also apply to the mind's complex non-linear system?

Information Theory says that DNA is a code before it's a protein. It's a lovely thought – power lies in immaterial codes which means, in effect, that non-matter rules matter. Or what about the undertones generated by the idea that complexity comes out of rule-governed simplicity? Rules drive the cosmos. Thought itself is also such a strange thing. How odd it is that thought should be. It's more extraordinary than the fact that thought can think up a God. Yet thought is the only thing known to exist. Nothing else can be, not even the things science deals with.

The early years of the 20th century also produced elegant ideas – Einstein's Quantum Theory, for instance, and Relativity. Time is a dimension like up and down and sideways? It's as plain as day, apparently, in the maths though no mathematician can visualise it, that being beyond the limits of the brain. Or what about the idea of James Jeans that the cosmos is a thought? Or Whitehead pointing out that there are no things – only processes and organisation? A table is a hierarchy from immaterial energy to solidity, as is the dinner and the diner seated at it, eating. Logic itself breaks down (All Cretans are liars) at a certain depth. Is that a comfort or not? Whatever it is, it's an undertone worth harbouring.

The concept of elegance is also an idea worth having. Theories which are elegant or beautiful in themselves are more likely to be right than ugly or clumsy ones. "Truth is beauty" as the anti-scientist Keats said, and "Beauty is Truth". $E=MC^2$ is elegance itself – at the speed of light matter and energy are one and the same.

Science has little to say about the mystic experience itself. Presumably it'd register on a brain scan if the experiencer were in NMR machine at the time the experience took place, an unlikely event. Mysticism isn't fortune telling, or the occult, or New Age, or a drug-bent mind, or charlatanism in sandals and beads. It can be quite respectable and suburban, bourgeois even. As has been said before, it's a life changing event and therefore of value although if science ever says it's wrong, then wrong it is. Mysticism comes when thought goes, but thought is a human essential. You can survive without mysticism, but not thought, though you need both to be fully human and alive.

Systems

The mystic experience occurs when the intellect momentarily stops functioning. It's therefore hard – impossible – for the intellect to fully understand what's going on. What's behind this inexplicable feeling of joy, peace, meaning, purpose, clarity, simplicity, and a sense of a goodness at the heart of things which makes people, generally speaking, bigger and better? Minor mystics, in particular, tend either to accept or mistake it for something else. For some, however, that isn't enough; they need theories and explanations, which they sometimes make up for themselves. 69

Auden (the post-War Christian Auden, that is, not the pre-War Marxist one) thought people have a Primary and a

Secondary Imagination. The Primary seems to be the mystic insight itself, common to all regardless of time or culture. The Secondary is what the intellect does with that insight after it's been filtered through the zeitgeist. Some people on the other hand are free of their day's dominant mindset and they tend to build systems of their own.

Plato (427-347 BC), the mystic, saw the changeless Good beyond the world of change. A philosopher, he believed, is anybody who's seen and been changed by it. Plato, the thinker, then went on to build a theoretical political system on top of it. How can philosophers help? By learning king-craft and becoming philosopher-kings to govern the perfect kingdom – in reality, a slave or totalitarian state. His attempts to set one up in the Greek colony of Syracuse in Italy came to nothing. Karl Popper, of the Open Society, blamed him for the 20th century's statist dictatorships, though seemingly unaware of Plato's mystical side. (Does it take one to know one?)

Plotinus (204-270), a Greek-speaking 3rd century Egyptian, studied philosophy in Alexandria for a dozen years before going off with Gordian III's army to Persia. He planned to travel on to India to talk to the gymnosophists, the naked philosophers who refused to let food and clothing interfere with thought. The Emperor, however, was killed by his own soldiers and Plotinus went to Rome instead. In his last few years (he died in his early sixties) he built a system on top of Plato's mystical insights which, sixteen hundred years later, came to be called Neo-Platonism, but which in the meantime had influenced early Christian theology. The cosmos, he taught, is an organism whose beating heart is God. God breathes in and out. Out-going breath becomes Over-Mind, then Soul, then Matter, then small-scale human souls wrapped in it. At first these little flesh-enclosed souls behave babyishly, running around excitedly. Soon, they want to go home. The only way is to retrace the steps of creation by following God's indrawn breath (in fact using standard mind-stilling tricks, or meditation techniques).

Origen (185-254) was around nineteen when Plotinus

was born. Plotinus has been the more influential but is of lesser value to the mild mystic. Origen, who was also Greek-speaking but probably not an ethnic Greek, was bishop of Caesarea where St Paul had been jailed. Whether Origen was a mystic or not is hard to say. The church never canonised him; he was bit heretical (all will be saved, he preached – a logical conclusion if God is in fact Love.) It was said he'd castrated himself because the Bible told him to. True or not, who knows? He certainly didn't take all the Bible literally. Therein, in fact, lies his interest to the common or garden mystic.

Mankind, he thought, can be sorted into two psychological types: abstract thinkers and concrete thinkers or what he called pneumatics and pistics. The question he asked was: 'how can Christianity satisfy pistics *and* mystics, concrete *and* abstract thinkers?' How, in other words, to reconcile Being and Becoming, unchangingness and change, the blood and dust of Judea with Plato's eternal serenity? Simple: spiritual truths don't have to be literally true or real. Christianity could work without a Resurrection or even an historical Jesus. What is a factual story to concrete thinkers is a spiritual truth to the abstract kind. People are part love, part matter. But Love is divine and therefore so are people because they too experience it. If you nail that combination of matter and love on a cross, one will survive because it's immortal – and so is, therefore, every person who has ever lived on earth. (Without a theory of evolution, he didn't have to say when this all began. Today, perhaps, he might have said with the rise of self-consciousness.) Origen also thought the second Coming had come – the Kingdom is within, something every minor mystic who ever lived can endorse.

Richard Jefferies, a Wiltshire farmer's son, was a novelist and nature writer whose life was short, poor, and sickly. TB killed him in 1887 when he was still only thirty-nine. If he's read now it's for his nature notes centred on Wiltshire, outer London (still fairly rural back then), and the southern counties. Like Shelley he was an atheist mystic, unusual in the West. Instead of a God he saw a Life Force, a blind thing

71

without feeling or consciousness. Sunshine to him was what moonlight was to Keats – it triggered mental shut down. One bright summer morning he stood on London Bridge and: "I felt in the midst of eternity then, in the midst of the supernatural, among the immortal; … and I knew the supernatural to be more intensely real than the sun." Which is a big thing to happen to anybody but for Jefferies it wasn't enough: he added a theory. Cavemen, he decided unilaterally, had had three Ideas: soul, immortality, the gods. He thought, of course, that there is no immortality, no soul, no gods – but thinking about them gives them a kind of life. But there's more, a Fourth Idea, his own discovery: Soul-Entity. If life is a thought, there's also a greater Cosmos of Thought beyond it. The Cavemen's three ideas are like a lake: his one idea is like the sea.

Blake was a far deeper mystic than Jefferies. At the age of four he saw God looking in at the window, and never looked back. A little later he saw "a tree filled with angels, bright angelic wings bespangling every bough like stars." Later still: "When the sun rises, do you not see a round disk of fire somewhat like a Guinea?" "Oh, no, no, I see an Innumerable host crying 'Holy, Holy, Holy, is the Lord God Almighty.'" It's said he sang with joy as he lay dying.

He was completely non-dualist – mankind is not a separate and inferior creation. All is God. All is one. Everybody is Christ. Man is divine. Ruination comes through concentration on little things and the self, mistaking them for the whole. All this, he argued, becomes clear when you see things properly: "If the doors of perception were cleansed everything would appear as it is, infinite." (By that, of course, he meant shutting down the intellect to let another reality break through.)

Imagination – or mystic vision as opposed to logic, science, self-centredness, materialism – links this world to the spiritual. Without it you have cruelty and selfishness. It's a vicious circle, a negative feedback loop: without mystic vision you can't feel for others, not feeling for others dulls mystic vision, with a dulled mystic vision you can't feel for others.

Love and understanding are the beginnings of change. "One must die for another through all eternity," he says, in order to break the stranglehold of selfhood, the only unredeemable sin.

So far, so wise. But that elegant insight is then lost in a private mythology of Urizen, Luvah, Enitharmon, Bromion, *The Book of Thel*, *The Book of Ahania*, *The Song of Los*. Cribs can make some sense of it all, though in the end nothing is to be gained by trying to.

Thomas Carlyle (1795-1881) didn't do God, either; he did a Force, encountered when he was twenty-six in a street in Edinburgh. It taught him that he, Thomas Carlyle, was divine. This made him fearless. Since everything's made of the Force, the Force can be reached through everything. Nothing dies. Matter is spiritual. Everything is important but Heroes are most important of all. They're Force's highest embodiment, sent to make the ordinary and the unheroic see the truth. To the post-20th century mind it sounds sinister: it's also the downside of mysticism – the intellect twisting elegant purity into ugly complexity.

Politics

In her book, *Mysticism in English Literature*, Caroline Spurgeon lists Edmund Burke (1729-1797) as a mystic. She gives no reason for saying so but, taking her at her word, it leads to a strange conclusion: mysticism underlies a major Western system of political thought – Burke's was one of the shaping minds of history and many people in England still call themselves Burkean Tories.

What evidence there is may well be in the book he wrote as a teenager (not yet nineteen): *Philosophical Enquiry into the Origin of our Ideas of the Sublime and the Beautiful.* (It was published in 1757, when he was twenty-eight.) The book revolves around two main ideas. To begin with, Burke was the first writer in English to realise that beauty is in the mind, not in the thing: in the perceiver, not the perceived. The

73

Sublime – Beauty's counterpart – is a response to terror or pain (or, better, astonishment and awe). It tightens the muscles, whereas pleasure from beauty softens them.

The second idea – and a most important one (although overlooked) – is that both the Sublime and the Beautiful work by stopping thought, closing down the mind – "all its motions are suspended" is the way he puts it. Inevitably, and invariably, from that will follow the mystic experience. Could Burke have known the cause and not the effect?

Unlike most lesser mystics he had a major effect on art and politics. Forty and fifty years later both Turner and Wordsworth made poetry and pictures out of these abstract ideas. One of Turner's paintings is called: *Snow Storm – Steam Boat off a Harbour's Mouth Making Signals in Shallow Water, and Going by the Lead. The Author was in this Storm on the Night the Ariel Left Harwich* (1842). The story used to be that Turner had had himself lashed to Ariel's foremast to experience a storm in all its Sublimity from the inside. (Disappointingly the story's now disputed.) Safe on the harbour wall, the spectator is shown the inner energy of a storm at sea as it engulfs a little paddle steamer in a colossal circle of unleashed fury. Fire belches from her tall funnel as the stoker strives to keep up a head of steam to give her steerage way. The smoke from her own thin funnel, too, is bent and curved into becoming part of the storm cloud – unrealistically, probably; more likely the wind would rip it apart and scatter it. All the same, this isn't realism – it's the essence of an experience cut out and presented as a thing in its own right.

Burke was an Irishman of Norman descent. His mother was a Catholic, his father an Anglican solicitor in Dublin where Edmund was born in 1729. He went from a Quaker school to Trinity College, Dublin. (The debating society he set up there still meets (the *Annual Register*, which he co-founded in 1758, survives as well).) He became a Middle Temple lawyer, but gave up the law to become a professional writer and then a politician. By the end of his life he'd been an MP for three constituencies, two of them Rotten

Boroughs. The other was Bristol. Bristolians failed to re-elect him when he stood by his principles in Parliament and refused to vote in their interest (to restrict Irish trade). His life was about the politics of justice. He supported the rebels in the American colonies, moved for the impeachment of Warren Hastings, and opposed the tyranny of the French Revolution (becoming an Old Whig as opposed to Fox's New revolution-loving ones). He died in 1797 of stomach cancer, before the Terror, Napoleon, and the long wars came along.

Why should he have inspired a strand of Toryism? The human species is a pack mammal with evolved self-consciousness and so can look two ways: to the pack or collective, to the individual. Mystics, high or low, tend not to be coercive collectivists. They see unity underlying all things, not uniformity imposed by emotionally driven ideas and a statist cast of mind. Burke, the Old Whig, wrote words which New Tories could live by, all the more deeply because they carry undertones.

"Among a people generally corrupt, liberty cannot long exist. Liberty too must be limited in order to be possessed. Never, no never, did Nature say one thing and Wisdom say another. Bad laws are the worst sort of tyranny. The people never give up their liberties but under some delusion. A state without the means of some change is without the means of its conservation. Good order is the foundation of all good things. Dangers by being despised grow great. Those who have been once intoxicated with power .. can never willingly abandon it.

And having looked to the government for bread, on the very first scarcity they will turn and bite the hand that fed them. When bad men combine, the good must associate; else they will fall, one by one, an unpitied sacrifice in a contemptible struggle. People will not look forward to posterity, who never look backward to their ancestors."

ELEVEN

A Long Defeat and a Failure

James Thomson (BV)

Where even the most minor mystic sees a fullness at the heart of things, James Thomson (1834-1882) saw only emptiness. To that extent he was a minus-mystic, it there can be such thing, an anti-mystic, living in a world without joy or any sense of something greater than the self, sunk in self-absorption and unrelievable pain. He's now mainly known as the author of a long poem, *The City of Dreadful Night*, an anthem for the lost. At its worst it's very bad; at it's best it's good and comforting to chronically sad people. Clinical depression or melancholia was once the English disease and the language had dozens of words for it; *vapours, spleen, fits of the mother, hypp, hypocons, moonpals, markambles, hockogrockles* among them. (Robert Burton's *The Anatomy of Melancholy* (1621) has a full list.)

"A long defeat" was how Thomson summed up of his life. He was born in Port Glasgow in 1834 and was only four when his father, a sailor, was paralysed by a stroke. Then the boy caught measles and infected his sister who died as a result. When his mother died he was sent to a military academy in London and then into the Army as a schoolmaster. He was court-martialled and dishonourably discharged, probably for being drunk all the time. Before then however he'd met Charles Bradlaugh, a trooper in the 7th Dragoon Guards, in barracks in Ireland. After leaving the Army Bradlaugh set up an atheist and republican magazine called *The National Reformer* and Thomson worked for him for time before going to Colorado to buy a gold mine (which he failed to do) for a London company. The *New York World* then hired him to

cover the Carlist army in the war in Spain. He never filed a
story but did get sun stroke and after six weeks was fired. Back
in London he worked for Bradlaugh again, as well as
freelancing for *Cope's Tobacco Plant*, a magazine for smokers,
and *The Secularist*, ditto for atheists. (Even Swinburne, a
fellow atheist, said a lot of what he wrote was silly and
childish. God is "a desperately sharp shaver and a terrible
fellow for going to law" may be a sentence Swinburne had in
mind.) His by-line was BV: B for Bysshe (Shelley), V for
Vanolis (an anagram of Novalis).

Drink and tobacco, both in large quantities, were his
drugs although they didn't help his chronic insomnia – often
he walked the streets of London all night. In his last two years
drink completely got the better of him. Once he locked
himself in a lavatory for six hours. Friends banned him from
their house; he'd been drunk all the time and even hid bottles
in the stump of a tree in their garden in Leicestershire. He set
fire to the kitchen in his lodgings in London and was had up
on an arson charge. He held up a corner shop kept by an old
lady; she knew him and didn't press charges. Another time he
held off three policemen in spite of being under five foot five
in height. Fines went unpaid until he was jailed for a
fortnight.

Either nicotine or alcohol could have done for him – in
the event a burst blood vessel got there first. A friend found
him lying on a bed in a lodging house. By the light of a match
he saw blood on the pillow. BV was taken by cab to University
College Hospital where be slowly bled to death over the next
couple of days, conscious to the last. He was forty seven.

The City of Dreadful Night is a city of the mind, but real:
a real unreal city. How people get there nobody knows: it's in
a roadless wilderness of mountains and moors lost in
perpetual night. Like all great cities it has a river, the River of
the Suicides, flowing into a shipless sea. From the hills, the
city is a nocturne in lead and faded gold: a line of faint light
marks where the city broods in its own endless night. In
daylight it shrinks till it's no bigger than a human heart
though it's always there, a place of despair peopled by a sad

brotherhood of monks and kings, priests, drunks, artists, poets, soldiers. And it is a brotherhood, with few women and fewer children. The elderly are also rare.

Those smudges of faded gold are lamps little brighter than the moon. By their light the poet follows the only man who seems to act with purpose yet he, too, merely circles wearily from where love died to where faith died to where hope died. Can there be life when these have gone? Only like a clock without a dial: it ticks, it works, it has no purpose or meaning.

Two men sit under an elm by the River of the Suicides. One speaks:

> The world rolls round for ever like a mill;
> It grinds out death and life and good or ill;
> It has no purpose, heart or mind or will.
> Man might know one thing were his sight less dim
> That it whirls not to suit his petty whim,
> That it is quite indifferent to him.

The narrator goes into the city's cathedral. Shafts of moonlight sift down like dust. A preacher speaks from the pulpit:

> My soul hath bled for you these sunless years,
> With bitter blood-drops running down like tears:
> Oh, dark, dark, dark, withdrawn from joy and light!
>
> And now at last authentic word I bring,
> Witnessed by every dead and living thing:
> Good tidings of great joy for you, for all: There is no
>   God.
>
> This little life is all we must endure,
> The grave's most holy place is ever sure,
> We fall asleep and never wake again.
>
> O Brothers of sad lives! they are so brief;
> A few short years must bring us all relief.

"What comfort can I find in this?" a voice cries out of the darkness, before going on to say:

In all eternity I had one chance,
One few years' term of gracious human life:
The splendour of the intellects advance,
The sweetness of the home with babes and wife.

My wine of life is poison mixed with gall,
My noonday passes in a nightmare dream.
I worse than lose the years which are my all.

The preacher replies:

My Brother, my poor Brothers, it is thus,
This life holds little good for us
But it ends soon and never more can be.
I ponder these things and they comfort me.

On the cold northern mountains above the city sits the statue of Melencolia (the usual illustration is Dürer's etching). She's slumped in thought – itself a block on minor mysticism – and, worse, absorbed in herself. So self-absorbed she's as good as blind.

Why betray the secrets of the City in this way? Thomson asks. Because there's a fellowship of the desolate and some sad, lost brother might read these words and be comforted, knowing he's not alone. Besides, it's no betrayal: the City's unknowable to outsiders. Only those who live there can ever know it. In this it's a bit like the mystic experience perhaps although, having said that, these two places are polar opposites. There are of course other reasons for clinical depression but one cause (or symptom) is ceaseless self-absorption. If the gates of the City of Dreadful Night are shut on the sufferer by thoughts of the self, those of the Celestial City open only when thought of every kind stops.

T S Eliot

The Four Quartets (1935/42), like *The Scholar Gipsy*, is a quest poem. Unlike Arnold, Eliot knew what he was looking for – a mystical experience – but not how to find it. He also had some idea of what it would be like: it was an insight into the singleness and unity underlying all things. Or as he put it at the end of *The Dry Salvages*, the last of the *Quartets*: "And the fire and the rose are one". In his play, *Murder in the Cathedral*, he makes Thomas à Beckett say:

> I have had a tremor of bliss, a wink of heaven, a
>   whisper,
> And I would no longer be denied; all things
> Proceed to a joyful consummation.

So why couldn't he find that 'tremor of bliss' or know from personal experience that the fire and the rose are one? He was a Victorian and an American, born in 1888 and brought up in St Louis, in the Mississippi valley, and on the New England coast. Cosseted by mother and sisters, he was an introverted boy with a hernia and so unable to do boyish things. (Not, perhaps, that he'd have wanted to any way.) He was unusually bookish – undergraduate at Harvard, post-graduate at the Sorbonne and Oxford (he was then twenty-six). He settled in London in 1914, became a British subject in 1927, and located himself on the spectrum of his new country as an Anglo-Catholic Monarchist Classicist. His first marriage to a mentally unstable woman was disastrous. She died in 1947 in a psychiatric hospital. They'd lived apart for fourteen years. His second marriage, in his old age, was – as far as it known – more serene. He earned a living successively as a teacher, banker, publisher, as well as being a successful magazine editor (his *Criterion* was important and influential) and one of the 20th century's most outstanding literary critics. He died in 1965, aged seventy-six. As a man, he was possibly a-sexual or at least virginal because of the hernia and its truss. He was dapper and always *looked* as if he should be wearing spats long after fashion abandoned them.

All of this adds up to a portrait of an up-tight intellectual, and which offers the simplest reason why he was a failed mystic – the unstoppability of his thoughts. He brings to mind a line from his own *Gerontion*: 'Thoughts of a dry brain in a dry season'. The *Four Quartets* are all about striving ("We shall not cease from exploration") and about how the undefeated keep on trying – whereas the only way is to let go, give in, surrender, free the mind of clutter. He was like a man buried alive and scrabbling to get out: except he was lying face down.

The Four Quartets also often read like something read, not lived. One passage in *East Coker*, is practically a paraphrase of *The Ascent of Mount Carmel* in which St John of the Cross describes the *via negativa*, the way to Divine union through negation. It's routine advice for would-be mystics – stop desiring or wanting anything for yourself. What it all boils down to is: "Stop thought". Eliot reproduces the saint's argument in what Hopkins would have called very Delphic verse (that is, the lowest kind). Three lines are enough:

> You must go by a way wherein there is no ecstasy,
> In order to arrive at what you do not know
> You must go by a way which is the way of ignorance

Later, in *Little Gidding*, Eliot talks of attachment and detachment – but again it's all very detached from personal experience. He then lifts the words of Julian of Norwich.

> All shall be well and all shall be well, and
> All manner of thing shall be well.

We have an exact date for Julian's mystical experience: 8th May 1373. She was thirty, a Benedictine nun, and an anchoress at St Julian's Church (hence her name) in Norfolk. She left an account of her experiences in a book, *Showings* (or what she was shown to her). People and God are one and the same, she says. The sense-soul doesn't know this because it's steeped in trivialities and the self. Sin isn't something you do. It's not a deed. It's the failure to be what we are meant to be. It's an absence of love. We know it only by the pain it causes. Pain is something however, and is a necessity; we need it for growth – without it there can be no bliss. God is love and so, although sin is permitted, it lasts for only a short while. God doesn't blame people for sin, nor is it something to be ashamed of. When He sees our sin, He pities the pain it causes and forgives. All of this, of course, is unorthodox and probably heretical as well, but it's true to the mystic's vision and not something Eliot knew at first hand.

The Waste Land (1921/22) is a lament for the decay of civilisation as Eliot saw it. Coming at the end of the Great War it found a ready readership in the university educated middle class particularly, it must be supposed, those too young to be have been in the trenches. Eliot was still irreligious when he wrote it although the title of the poem is from the Arthurian cycle about the search for the Holy Grail which will cure the groin-hurt Fisher-King and bring the kingdom back to health. The land is wasted by spiritual, not material, decay and the Holy Grail is spirituality, or perhaps even the mystic experience which, later in life, Eliot wanted but never got. The ending of *The Wasteland*. is bookish and unfelt – three words taken from the Sanskrit of the *Upanishads*: "give, sympathise, control". They, too, have the feeling of something recently read and dropped in, not something internalised.

From a minor mystic's point of view, some of his very early, pre-*Wasteland*, work is more interesting. In it there's a sadness – but the sadness of emptiness, not for the loneliness of things. *The Love Song of J. Alfred Prufrock* (1910/11) and *Portrait of a Lady* (1910/11) are studies in acedia, melancholy, and the sloth of the spiritually dead. This, in fact, is depression, not sadness. Yet, oddly enough, *Prufrock* (at least) can create lasting undertones out of the essential sadness of things, in this case of human life itself.

> For I have known them all already, known them all
> Have known the evenings, mornings, afternoons
> I have measured out my life in coffee spoons;
> I know the voices dying with a dying fall
> Beneath the music from a farther room.
>   So how should I presume?
>
>   In the room the women come and go
>   Talking of Michelangelo.

Should I, after tea and cakes and ices,
Have the strength to force the moment to its crisis?

I have heard the mermaids singing ...
I do not think that they will sing to me.

I have seen them riding seaward on the waves,
Combing the white hair of the waves blown back
When the wind blows the water white and black.

> I grow old ... I grow old ...
> I shall wear the bottoms of my trousers rolled.

Prufrock is set in St Louis, Missouri, where Eliot grew up. (He took the name from the shop front of a furniture store owned by a Mr Prufrock.) *Portrait of a Lady* is set on Beacon Hill in Boston and the name of the lady is known: Adeline Moffat. In his autobiography Conrad Aitken calls her "the *précieuse ridicule* to end all preciocity, serving tea so exquisitely among her bric-à-brac". In the poem she's caught just as cruelly in an analysis of the spiritually dead; she's the lady of friendships, all ache and emptiness, the loneliness of disconnection. It's an insight into a life that appals by its vacuity and pretension. It stays in the mind like Thomson's *The City of Dreadful Night* as something that diminishes life, the antithesis of great art.

TWELVE

Adolescent Undertones?

Why is A E Housman (1859-1936) still so popular? His simple poetry of beer, betrayal, and death on the edge of Empire went out of fashion years ago yet *A Shropshire Lad*, first published in 1896, is still on sale on open shelves in bookstores where poetry is stocked in out of the way alcoves because it sells so badly. Housman has upset people (enraged intellectuals, more accurately) ever since. Auden called him adolescent. Orwell claimed he was read by public schoolboys tormented by deviant house masters. Cyril Connolly said (a) he was unclassical and (b) he was "emotionally vulgar and shallow" and so of course appealed to adolescents who fondly remembered him thereafter.

None of these men – Housman included – was in the least mystical. (Auden was drawn to Anglicanism by ritual.) Orwell was a socialist materialist, and Connolly was something similar. If each blamed the immaturity of late childhood for Housman's popularity, Connolly was perhaps the closest to a truth. What did young people get out of his poetry? An uplift of some kind? In which case it probably generates undertones. In memory most of his verse seems to be about blue hills and landscape – in fact comparatively little of it is: undertones may account for the false memory. In which case, also, it passes the Ruskin test: "Does this make people bigger and better?" At one stage of life (if the above trio are right) the answer is 'yes'. Borderline good work can do that, yet there always seems to be more to Housman.

His surface emotions are simple, his words easy to understand, and often there's a sadness, a nostalgia for the things that are no more (even youth seems to feel the pull of this).

Into my heart an air that kills
From yon far country blows:
What are those blue remembered hills,
What spires, what farms are those?

That is the land of lost content,
I see it shining plain,
The happy highways where I went
And cannot come again.

For many people back in those days, although clearly not
all, to be English was to feel you had a spiritual home.
Housman evoked that feeling. He can also, therefore, be read
as a poet of patriotism. Frank Harris annoyed him by
assuming Housman shared his opinions and mocked Queen,
country, and the King's Shropshire Light Infantry in his
poetry. 'I didn't, and I don't,' Housman told him, angrily. It's
hard to know what to make of him: as a gay man at the time
of Wilde's trial he had no reason to feel affection for his own
country. The first thing he did in the Great War (he was in his
mid-fifties, too old to enlist) was to give most of his money to
the Exchequer, but then he seems to have ignored young
soldiers, wounded or under orders for the Front, who were
billeted in his college in Cambridge. The War often seemed
to be an annoyance to him – except in 1915 when he was able
to go to the Riviera without the usual appalling people, as he
called them, being there. Next year annoyance was back: he
refused to take the ferry to Le Havre when the military port of
Dieppe was closed to all but troopships. He had a strange
blindness about what was happening in Flanders – he once
said things would be back to normal after the War, when of
course nothing has ever been the same since and which must
have been obvious at the time. Was he an introvert to whom
the inner was reality, the outer scarcely real at all?

A Shropshire Lad sold well in the Great War. For some –
soldiers at the Front, in particular – Housman created a
landscape capable of evoking Englishness, a country in the
soul. His Shropshire may be mythical but myth tells a truth
that can't always be told in any other way. The unmystical

miss all this and, if they're intellectuals, come up with far-fetched theories to explain him. Speaking about *On Wenlock Edge*, one critic invoked the atomic theory of Democritus as filtered through Epicurus and Lucretius: the Roman at Wenlock Edge, in this scenario, was a collocation of atoms broken down and reassembled as a Victorian yeoman.

On Wenlock Edge, more simply, is about continuity and time. An English farmer watching a gale in the woods on the short range of hills called Wenlock Edge is moved by an intuition that a Roman soldier must have seen this exact sight long ago, and that the thoughts and the troubles of both are the same, unchangingly human in the middle of change.

> On Wenlock Edge the wood's in trouble;
> His forest fleece the Wrekin heaves;
> The gale, it plies the saplings double,
> And thick on Severn snow the leaves.
>
> 'Twould blow like this through holt and hanger
> When Uricon the city stood:
> 'Tis the old wind in the old anger,
> But then it threshed another wood.
>
> Then, 'twas before my time, the Roman
> At yonder heaving hill would stare:
> The blood that warms an English yeoman,
> The thoughts that hurt him, they were there.

Sadness – the loneliness of time, place, and things – are embedded in Housman:

> On the idle hill of summer,
> Sleepy with the flow of streams,
> Far I hear the steady drummer
> Drumming like a noise in dreams.

And:

> In summertime on Bredon
> The bells they sound so clear;
> Round both the shires they ring them
> In steeples far and near.

Housman was born in 1859 in Worcestershire with the Clee Hills of Shropshire on the western horizon. His mother died of cancer on his twelfth birthday: by his thirteenth he was a deist; a few years later he became the atheist he remained all his life. He knew of nothing beyond the material, yet was also the man who devised the shaving test for poetry. Each morning when shaving he'd prop his latest verse by the mirror. If the razor slid easily, the poetry was good because his whiskers stood on end – a physical response to beauty but not a spiritual one?

Housman was narrow – narrowed farther than nature intended, perhaps, by failure and rejection. At Oxford he fell in love for the first and only time. Housman was gay; Moses Jackson wasn't – he was a beefy rowing blue up in Oxford on a science scholarship. Homosexuality he called 'beastliness' or 'spooniness'. Housman wrote:

Because I liked you better
Than suits a man to say,
It irked you and I promised
To throw the thought away.

His problem was he never did throw the thought away. If you think you've loved more than once, he'd say, you haven't loved at all.

And if you'd asked him the great Socratic question: 'How should we live?' he'd have said: 'Through knowledge for its own sake, curiosity, the craving to know things as they really are.' As an undergraduate in Oxford in the 1870s he already knew what his life's work was to be: redaction – the search for truth through correcting scribal errors in classical texts. He made his name with his edition of Manilius, a 1st century Roman astronomer whose poetry was poor, whose science was poorer. To Housman, the quality of the book as literature didn't matter. All that did was the accuracy of the text – what did the writer write, how did scribes miscopy it? Truth was paramount and was to be found in exact knowledge. Somewhere hidden in the errors of a classical text was the truth – the very words the poet had written. To find them again was to right a kind of wrong. Redaction was also therefore about the defeat of decay. The Tree of Knowledge will make us wise, he argued, because our natures need knowledge to be fulfilled.

Housman's verses are unique, unique also in their undertones and uneasy mystic allure. Music adds nothing to them although there was a fashion in the early 20th century for setting him to music: dozens of composers tried – Butterworth, Ireland, Gurney, Bax, Bliss and Vaughan Williams among them. Housman never liked it (he was a-musical to begin with) but of them all he disliked Vaughan Williams the most. None (Vaughan Williams included) pulled it off. His high notes are out of place, disrupting the quietness of this kind of verse which was never intended for a baritone at the top of his register.

Vaughan Williams begins his setting of *Is my team ploughing* with a simple violin tune which is not just fine but very beautiful – until it reaches the words when it spoils both itself and them. The same tune is repeated like a refrain between verses; it has unexploited possibilities. The conceit is that a dead man is questioning his still living friend. The final question is:

> Is my friend hearty,
> Now I am thin and pine,
> And has he found to sleep in
> A better bed than mine?
>
> Yes, lad, I lie easy,
> I lie as lads would choose;
> I cheer a dead man's sweetheart,
> Never ask me whose.

The music at the end is even more out of keeping, over-loud, over-dramatic, urgent where the words suggest quietness, and a kind of regret rather than slyness. Vaughan Williams, the mystic, missed the point of the unmystical Housman.

Evocations of a landscape which Housman never

actually described stay as undertones deep in the mind. He had some of the makings of a mild mystic and was an undertone-maker to a rare degree. Nothing about him quite seems to fit.

THIRTEEN

The Mystic Century

Blake, Wordsworth, Coleridge, Shelley, Keats, Palmer, Carlyle, Mr and Mrs Browning, D G and C Rossetti, Emily Brontë, Coventry Patmore, Tennyson, Thompson, Jefferies, Meredith, Ruskin, Hopkins, Newman, Chesterton, Holst, Rupert Brooke, Evelyn Underhill, Buchan, Masefield, Vaughan Williams. Also: F C Happold, J W Rowntree, Henry Martyn,

All these people were mystics – mainly lesser ones – who lived at least part of their lives in the 19th century (that materialist age of steam and expansion), most of them also in the reign of Queen Victoria. The 19th was, by a long chalk, the most mystical century in all English history. (From the wider English-speaking world you can also add Walt Whitman, Emerson, and the American Transcendentalists.)

Caroline Spurgeon's *Mysticism in English Literature* (1913) deals with many of them. Some she missed. Hopkins hadn't been published at the time, while Chesterton and Vaughan Williams hadn't yet made their names. But passing over Ruskin and Newman is odd. Otherwise she can rarely be bettered, particularly for her definition of the mystic vision: "unity underlies diversity".

Spurgeon had a particular soft spot for Blake. To her he was world class, far out-ranking his fellow-countrymen in the global league table. He was, she seemed to think, almost worth all the other English mystics put together. "He outsoars them all," she claimed, "and includes them all. He possessed .. a philosophy, a system, and a profound scheme of the universe revealed to him in a vision." Furthermore: "He lived in a world of glory, of spirit, and of vision which for him was the only real world."

Part of Blake's attraction might have been been political

since he'd been angry about the social conditions of late Georgian England, and Victorians of Spurgeon's cast of mind and generation were still getting angry about them in their own time.

> Is this a holy thing to see
> In a rich and fruitful land,
> Babes reduc'd to misery,
> Fed with cold and usurous hand?

"The real evil," Spurgeon goes on, "is that we can suffer the need of the crust of bread to exist. This is a view which is gradually beginning to be realised today." She wasn't entirely right – Ruskin's *Unto This Last*, which led to the Welfare State, had been published half a century earlier. LLoyd George's Liberal Government had already, in 1908, introduced state pensions for the over seventies (between one and five shillings a week). Whether Blake would agree with nationalised compassion, of course, we can never know, but mystics are rarely collectivists – it's ruled out by the nature of their experience. He also said: "He who would do good to another must do it in minute particulars. General good is the plea of the scoundrel." She ends her account of Blake with a couplet:

> If the Sun and Moon should Doubt
> They would immediately go out.

"Mystics," says Spurgeon, "are the only people in the world who are 'possessors of certainty'. They have seen, they have felt; what need they of further proof? Logic, philosophy, theology are empty sounds and barren forms to those who know." What Blake knew gave rise to a few quotations useful to the semi-mystic:

> This life's five windows of the soul
> Distorts the heavens from pole to pole,
> And leads you to believe a lie
> When you see with, not thro', the eye.

"If the doors of perception were cleansed everything would appear as it is, infinite."

"A fool sees not the same tree that wise man does."

Percy Bysshe Shelley (1792-1822) was only thirty when he died. He was an atheist whose belief in the Suffering Love which is incarnate in humanity sounds rather Christian. Death, he thought, is a door which will open to show you the truth of this. That's pretty Christian too. Where he differed most strongly was in believing people are perfectible in the here and now. All they need is Will because Love and Imagination between them can build utopia. It's a mystic's insight plus a young man's wishful thinking. This belief that human nature is plastic and alterable by an act (of somebody else's) will led twentieth century Marxists, in part at least, to claim him as a proto-one-of-their-own, unaware of his mysticism which is as far from dialectical materialism as you can get.

John Keats (1795-1821) had, for the lesser mystic, a more timeless lesson – a formula, in fact, like $E=MC^2$: "Beauty = Truth, Truth = Beauty" (B=T. T=B.) Truth is the unchanging unity below the diversity of matter, and so is Beauty. The two are aspects of the same thing.

D G Rossetti (1828-1882), according to Spurgeon, was besotted not so much with generalised beauty as with particular beautiful female faces. To him they symbolised love which in turn cleared up the mystery of the meaning of life. Unfortunately (Spurgeon suggests) he got bogged down in the purely physical and missed out on the spiritual. In that he sounds very 21st century.

Spurgeon calls Emily Brontë (1818-1848) "one of the most strange and baffling figures in our literature" – a woman whose life was bounded by a graveyard and the moors where the wind, in those days before the end of the Little Ice Age, wuthered. Philosophy, metaphysics, and the mystics themselves must have been unknown to her. All the same, apart from her novel *Wuthering Heights*, she also wrote mystical poetry recording the "vision of a soul." She knew that material things are valueless and that true reality lies below them. In *The Prisoner*, she tells of the ecstasy and freedom she experiences every night when a messenger brings "eternal liberty,/a hush of peace – a soundless calm."

Coventry Patmore (1823-1896) is little read nowadays, mainly perhaps because he's not very readable. His most famous poem, *Angel in the House*, is about his wife. He turned the simple 'unity under diversity' insight into a complex Swedenborgian system which seems to boil down to the idea that God is knowable through wedded bliss.

In the 18th and 19th centuries, Swedenborg was an influence on many, including Coleridge, Blake, and also Mrs Browning (1806-1861). She was attracted by his idea of correspondence: whatever happens here in the material world has a counterpart in the spiritual one. Spurgeon quotes a passage of very bad poetry – garbled prose, in fact – from Mrs Browning's verse novel about a woman called *Aurora Leigh*:

> There's not a flower of spring
> That dies in June, but vaunts itself allied
> By issue and symbol, by significance
> And correspondence, to that spirit-world
> Outside the limits of our space and time,
> Whereto we are bound.

Swedenborg's best idea – in the sense that it's still useful – is that love is the soul. Through love therefore the living can know something of immortality. It also makes the concept of the soul intelligible – as well as being, of course, the essence of Christianity.

Mrs Browning's husband, Robert (1812-1889) was, according to Spurgeon, one of the deepest of the English mystics. She doesn't say why. Nowadays he's more famous for eloping with Mrs B than for his verse which is little read, and wasn't all that popular in his lifetime, either. He's a difficult poet who is never going to be of use to the semi-mystic: nothing in his work shuts down the mind, nothing raises an undertone. *The Ring and the Book* is a twenty thousand line account in verse of a 17th century Roman murder case told in twelve books, ten of them from the point of view of people involved (the old game of how differently different people report the same event).

His philosophy, based on his mysticism, is of interest

when it's sieved out of the heaps of words which hide it. Love is where God and mankind meet; the purpose of life is to grow until they've met. Everything grows. As humans grow, they feel for all creation. Don't trust knowledge, but do trust love springing from an empty mind (which is a perfect summary of mysticism in all its strong or weak varieties). There's more to life than what we know through the senses. The physical eye sees material things but not the immaterial out of which the eyes themselves are made.

Browning was always big on villainy: his dramatic monologues are full of uninviting characters, and for a reason – the good can't exist without the bad.

> Only by looking low, ere looking high,
> Comes penetration of the mystery.

Life is a probation, a starting point. We're here to turn stumbling blocks into stepping stones. Pain is good because it makes you grow, although he himself was forced to get by without it, never having suffered over-much either in England or in Tuscany where he lived comfortably.

The British Library has a recording, made at a dinner party, of his reciting – and forgetting – his verse. He pronounces verses 'varses' in a drawling upper crust kind of way, though he was distinctly middle class by birth: his father was a Bank of England clerk.

Francis Thompson (1859-1907) was middle class, too; his father was a doctor, and a Catholic, in a Lancashire where recusancy had lingered on since the Reformation. He failed to become either a priest or a doctor and ended addicted to laudanum, sleeping rough on the streets of London. Then he sent some poems to Wilfrid Meynell, editor of the Catholic literary magazine, *Merry England*. The return address was the Charing Cross Post Office. Meynell delayed replying for three months, by when his letter was undeliverable. Instead, he printed one of Thompson's poems, which brought the poet himself to his office. It was the turning point in Thompson's life and he became quite fêted. Contemporaries compared him to Crashaw.

He called the unity underlying diversity "the many-splendoured thing" and he blames people squarely for being unable to see it.

'Tis ye, 'tis your estranged faces,
That miss the many-splendoured thing.

That's a quotation from *In No Strange Land*, a poem unpublished in his lifetime (and badly in need of revision). Apart from that, he's probably best known today for the title of a poem– *The Hound of Heaven* – the story of the spirit of a man in full flight from where he belongs. The hound, never mentioned in the body of the poem, is God. And yet at the same time the divine is in all things – disturb a flower and you trouble a star. God is everywhere and so everywhere is holy – even the arches of Charing Cross railway viaduct where homeless people slept rough. When your problems become unbearable, call out to God, and

                ... on thy so sore loss
Shall shine the traffic of Jacob's ladder
Pitched betwixt Heaven and Charing Cross.

Evelyn Underhill (1875-1941) was always a niche writer, her subject being mysticism. She was one herself, although influenced by Friedrich von Hügel, an Austrian Baron of the Holy Roman Empire who lived most of his life in England and was yet another system builder. Underhill's most famous book, *Mysticism* (1911), is still read. She thought it odd that so few Protestants have been mystics. (At the highest level, she clearly means.) On the other hand, is that so strange, given that Protestantism is about he spoken word and the intellect, whereas mysticism is about the emptied mind? In a later book, *Mystics of the Church* (1925), she mentions two 19th century English Protestants. Henry Martyn (1781-1812) was a hypersensitive and scholarly Cornishman who improbably became a missionary in India. He translated the New Testament into Urdu, Arabic, and Farsi. When bad health forced him to leave India he went to Iran to meet scholars and present his Farsi Bible to the Shah. He died on his way home at Tokat, a town in Turkey some miles from the sea. John Wilhelm Rowntree (1868-1905) was a Quaker chocolate maker from York. Told he was going blind, he "felt the love of God wrap him about" and "the whole soul flooded with light and love ... unspeakable peace." On the whole there's little in Underhill's book for the lesser mystic – her unspoken assumption is that mysticism is rare whereas in its milder forms it probably isn't. A mild form, as already argued, may be an evolutionary necessity. The unresolved question is why was there so much of it, particularly among articulate and educated people, in the 19th – the least likely – century?

FOURTEEN

The Minor Mystic's Manual

"Wordsworth was not only a poet, he was also a seer, a mystic and a practical psychologist with an amazingly subtle mind, and an unusual capacity for feeling; he lived a life of excitement and passion, and he preached a doctrine of magnificence and glory. It was not the beauty of Nature which brought him joy and peace, but the life in Nature. He himself had caught a vision of that life, he knew it and felt it, and it transformed the whole of existence for him. He believed that every man could attain this vision which he so fully possessed, and his whole life's work took the form of a minute and careful analysis of the processes of feeling in his own nature, which he left as a guide for those who would tread the same path. It would be correct to say that the whole of his poetry is a series of notes and investigations devoted to the practical and detailed explanation of how he considered this state of vision might be reached."

Caroline Spurgeon,
Mysticism in English Literature (1913)

There was a cross over point in Wordsworth's life: He was a mystic before he was a poet and a poet when no longer a mystic. His best work was done when both came together for the ten years between 1798 and 1808, or roughly the ages of twenty-eight to thirty-eighty. (His dates are 1770-1850.)

His poetry is a lower mystic's manual – almost all you need to know is here: mind-stopping passages, undertones, descriptions of what the mystic state is like, what causes it, its importance. (It's outdated only when he uses 18th century psychology to explain things.) His major work, *The Prelude*, is one of the purest and straightest accounts of nature mysticism in English. It's long – fourteen books at its longest

97

– but many shorter pieces are just as good and more immediate. This is from *Ode: Intimations of Immortality*:

> There was a time when meadow, grove, and stream,
> The earth, and every common sight,
> To me did seem
> Apparelled in celestial light.

Lines Written a Few Miles Above Tintern Abbey, on Revisiting the Banks of the Wye During a Tour, July 31st 1798 (usually, and understandably, shortened to *Tintern Abbey*) is the essence of mysticism itself caught in words. Turner had been there four years earlier. He painted the Abbey's soaring roofless arches with trees growing on the keystones, a great shaft of sunlight and tiny figures – two men, two women – barely visible in the vast ruined stone skeleton of the place. In the foreground, a wheelbarrow lies on its side, what it was carrying tipped out. Homeless people lived there, each family in their own niche-home. The poem itself, on the other hand, is less about the Abbey, more about the Wye valley, deep and green, winding down to the Severn. The geography scarcely matters; a description of the essence of the mystical experience does:

> And I have felt
> A presence that disturbs me with the joy
> Of elevated thoughts; a sense sublime
> Of something far more deeply interfused,
> Whose dwelling is the light of setting suns,
> And the round ocean and the living air,
> And the blue sky, and in the mind of man:
> A motion and a spirit that impels
> All thinking things, all objects of all thought
> And rolls through all things.

He began *The Prelude* in Germany in 1797 but wrote the bulk of it in Dove Cottage in Westmorland between 1799 and 1805, almost the beginning and the end years of his greatest period. Throughout the 1820s and '30s he altered and toned it down so as not to upset the pious, as he out it, and to conform to Anglican orthodoxy. He was sixty-nine when he finished, having worked on it intermittently for forty years. His widow published it in 1850 and gave it its title, because that's what it was – a prelude to a never written philosophical work on Man, Nature, and Society. *The Prelude* was to be his credentials, his authority to write the longer piece. The 1805 manuscript wasn't published until 1926 when the de Selincourt edition printed both versions in parallel. The 1799 copy didn't appear in print until 1959, a full hundred and sixty years after it was begun. *The Prelude* thus by-passed Romanticism, appearing in the same year as the purely Victorian but also mystically-tinged *In Memoriam.*

In all the years it was in manuscript, it never had a title. Among family and friends it was called *Poem to Coleridge* (which it was) or *Poem on the Growth of the Poet's Mind* – which it wasn't; it's a chronicle of decline from high level mystical spirituality to barrenness. A sub-theme is about shoring fragments against his ruin (to half quote T S Eliot). It was unique at the time: nobody had ever written about themselves so much and in such a way. (Perhaps nobody still has?)

In it, his mysticism can be traced from boyhood to young manhood. In Book 5 he talks about his return to Hawkshead in the long Cambridge vacation. One early morning he walked home after an all-night party:

> The sea was laughing at a distance; all
> The solid mountains were bright as clouds,
> Grain-tinctured, drenched in empyrean light;
> And in the meadows and the lower grounds
> Was all the sweetness of a common dawn -
> Dews, vapours, and the melody of birds,
> And labourers going forth into the fields.
> Ah, need I say, dear friend, that to the brim
> My heart was full? I made no vows, but vows
> Were then made for me; bond unknown to me
> Was given, that I should be – else greatly sinning -
> A dedicated spirit. On I walked
> In blessedness, which even yet remains.

In boyhood he'd been at one with a the cosmos in which there was no created, no creator, because all were equally uncreated:

> ... in all things
> I saw one life, and felt that it was joy.

Here he's talking about the 'interior life'...

> In which all beings live with God, themselves
> Are God, existing in one mighty whole,
> As indistinguishable as the cloudless East
> At noon is from the cloudless West, when all
> The hemisphere is one cerulean blue.

As with most people, sight was his dominant sense, but sound could work too (apparently he had little sense of smell). He recalls evenings by Windermere when he'd imitate the call of an owl on cupped hands. Owls all around the lake called back; he'd egg them on into wild hooting and echoes. Then they'd stop. In that silence, the outer world slid inside him and he became one with it.

People, like nature, were a gateway to the Beyond – particularly (or perhaps only) the rugged, the damaged, the solitary, the abandoned, the hurt, the old (who hear eternity calling). Each is like a quiet force of nature. (His own happiness, he said, let him look at 'painful things' without flinching. "We all of us have one human heart.") Several of his characters stay in the mind as undertones. Michael the shepherd, for example, the son of whose old age went to the bad and fled the country. Or the Idiot Boy galloping under the moon which he mistook for the sun grown cold.

Above all there's the leech-gatherer. A traveller is crossing a high moor on a bright morning after a night of storm. (There's a nice snapshot of a hare carrying a glittering mist of water around her paws as she races in the sun (is it March?)) The traveller meets an old man who makes his living collecting leeches from ponds and selling them, presumably, to doctors.

> From pond to pond he roamed, from moor to moor;

Housing, with God's good help, by choice or chance;
And in this way he gained an honest maintenance.

We remember Housman for landscapes he never described; we remember *The Leech-gatherer* for qualities Wordsworth never specifically gives the old man. If at a higher level people are both human and divine, at a lower one they're both human and elemental. The leech-gatherer is a bit of the landscape – not *like* a bit of the landscape, but an actual part of it, like a rock left behind by a glacier or ice sheet. (In the poem, Wordsworth likens him to a beast which has crawled out of the sea.) He's a man simplified almost to the inorganic, yet at the same time he has courtesy, grace, and gentleness. He's bent double with age and hardship after a rough life in wild places, and yet he's well-spoken:

Choice word and measured phrase, above the reach
Of ordinary men; a stately speech.

For some people words themselves can trigger the mystic event. (Perhaps they did for Hopkins who collected them: "grind, gride, gird, grit, groat, grate, greet...creak, croak, crake, graculus, crackle", as we read in his notebooks). Perhaps it was the same for Wordsworth though the evidence is scanty and inconclusive. But he did argue that a ...

......Visionary Power
Attends upon the motions of the winds
Embodied in the mystery of words.

As a boy at Hawkshead he'd walk in the early mornings with a friend reciting poetry together (Gray, mainly it seems, and Goldsmith). In words he found "a passion and a power".

He believed that poets should – must – 'see things as they are', and in this he pre-Ruskin'd Ruskin. *Is*, *are*, *am*, *be*, are important words in Wordsworth because what mystics see, or believe they see, is Being itself. 'Am' and 'Being' are the same thing because ultimately all is one. There is only Being and each human being is an aspect of it, cut off from knowing it by the inbuilt limitations of the brain. The fact of being, of existing, of existence, is itself also astonishing. Wordsworth often conflates disparate things into a kind of singleness. For example:

The silence that is the starry sky

where the connecting 'is' could be italicised to indicate that stars and silence are the same.

Motion is another important Wordsworthian word. Today, perhaps, we can (mentally at least) replace it with 'energy'? God for instance is …

… a motion and a spirit that impels
All thinking things, all objects of all thought,
And rolls through all things.

It can be read as 'God is an energy which impels all thinking things'. Also: 'motion of delight' equals 'energy of delight', or that tingling electric feeling of joy?

A sense of under-ness is common to all levels of mystics because the only important things do seem to be underneath material reality. Wordsworth coined 'under-soul', though it's not all that clear what he meant; the unconscious, perhaps (a word introduced into English by Coleridge from the German of Schelling). 'Soul-ness' is another Wordsworth coinage: he seems to have meant 'spiritual' by it. Great minds, he says, are 'exalted by an underpresence'. Later, he changed this to 'unconsciousness' but a passage in *The Prelude* makes it plain he meant a sense of the presence of God:

A meditation rose in me that night
Upon the lonely Mountain when the scene
Had pass'd away, and it appear'd to me
The perfect image of a mighty Mind,
Of one that feeds upon infinity,
That is exalted by an underpresence,
The sense of God, or whatsoe'er is dim
Or vast in its own being.

102

Of the two, Coleridge was the philosopher, Wordsworth (to some extent) the follower. To explain how poetry and mysticism work they used the psychology of the day. Consciousness, said Locke, is made up of incoming sense data added to data already collected and stored. Fresh incoming data fire off memories and together they create something new. David Hartley, writing in 1749, used this associationist theory to show how people learn about God and morality. Fear, which leads to the avoidance of wrong-doing, is implanted in the memory by the Sublime. Beauty teaches virtue. Nature implants feelings of warmth towards humanity, leading in some way to theopathy or an experience of God.

Ideas like these mean nothing today. Nevertheless, Wordsworth was influenced by them. In *The Prelude* he says:

Fair seed-time had my soul, and I grew up,
Fostered alike by beauty and by fear.

Hartley's was a mechanical clockwork-like cosmos and Coleridge (and Wordsworth following him) modified it in favour of something more in keeping with the mystic's view of things. Their cosmos was a living, creative Mind. People are creative because they have access to it: the human mind taps into this creativity through Imagination. Primary Imagination rearranges incoming sense data into daily reality. According to Coleridge, Secondary Imagination is what today would be called creativity of the kind which paints paintings or writes novels. For example, a group of people are standing on a beach – primary Imagination creates the world they, hear, see, feel, and smell: a gull calling, a breeze bringing the scent of kelp ashore. Secondary Imagination then turns the scene into a second creation – poetry, painting, or music. Wordsworth, on the other hand, thought one Imagination is enough because it reaches down to all levels of creativity – sensitive people use it to see their dinners and to see "into the life of things". People have mystic experiences because they can tap into the Ultimate Creativity which, to a Christian, is God.

He lays all this out, none too clearly, in *The Prelude*. One night Wordsworth and two friends climbed Snowdon in

103

order to be on the summit in time to see the sun rise. The lower slopes were covered by a thick mist. Standing above the mist was like being on the shores of a white sea which filled the bays of the hills and stretched away over the real ocean. A full moon shone in a clear sky. Silence and sound were there together. The noise was of streams pouring down the mountains under the sea-cloud. He felt he was in the presence of a living mind which 'feeds upon infinity'. Anybody, everybody, would have sensed Eternity that night on Snowdon but 'higher minds' create those experiences all the time out of more ordinary things.

How can matter know non-matter, how can the physical see the unphysical? Wordsworth wondered about these things as well but had no answer. "What is this mysticism?"he also asked. Sensibly, he said he didn't know while insisting *something* happens and therefore whatever it is, it exists: it is.

> I guess not what this tells of Being past,
> Nor what it augurs of the life to come,
> *But so it is.*

The experience is also priceless. People who know "the joy of the pure principle of love" are never again content with anything less. They look for 'kindred love' and 'kindred joy'. The things which prompt the experience "excite not morbid passions, no disquietude, no vengeance and no hatred." In this, again, he pre-Ruskin'd Ruskin.

He also worked out how it's done – by clearing the mind of "little enmities and low desires" until a "wise passiveness" or "happy stillness of mind" is arrived at. Nothing is too big or small to make it happen – from people to love, from dust and grit to landscape. Once, while crossing the Alps, he suddenly knew that "our being's heart and home is with infinitude" and that this knowledge comes

> ... when the light of sense
> Goes out, but with a flash that has revealed
> The invisible world.

During the Peninsular War, he and Coleridge used to

walk to Dunmail Raise to meet the cart which brought the newspapers. Wordsworth often put his ear to the ground to listen for the rumble of the cart wheels. One evening, as he got up, he noticed a star over Helvellyn. It triggered a "sense of the infinite". Why? Because of relaxation following concentration, was his answer. This also is true.

How did he sum up mysticism? "Central peace subsisting at the heart of endless agitation." Busyness with the material world is a mysticism blocker, he realised. "The world is too much with us" he wrote in a sonnet in 1806; all this "getting and spending" leads nowhere. And, once again he was pre-Ruskin in regretting the passing of the spirituality of the Greeks who saw gods in woods. We all need to

Have sight of Proteus rising from the sea;
Or hear old Triton blow his wreathed horn.

He was born in Cockermouth, a small Cumberland sea port, in 1770. His father, a lawyer, was factor to the Sir James Lowther who was later raised to the peerage as the Earl of Lonsdale. They were the Lonsdales of the boxing belt who still own the castle above the gorge at a bend in the River Lowther, a tributary of the Eden. The first noble earl cheated Wordsworth senior of four thousand pounds of wages. The second handed over the stolen money but only after being sued by the Wordsworth family, their father being dead by then.

William was the only one of her five children whose future his mother worried about. John, captain of the merchantman, *Earl of Abergavenny*, drowned when his ship was wrecked on the Shambles off Portland Bill in 1805. Christopher, the youngest, became Master of Trinity College, Cambridge, and the University's Vice-Chancellor. Richard, the oldest, was a lawyer like their father. Dorothy, a year younger than William (they were baptised at the same time) was to be his life's companion, even after his own marriage. Dorothy, too, was a writer (her diaries have since been published) with her brother's eye for nature though not, in all probability, his mystic instinct.

Their mother died when William was eight. Their father (who died only five years later) was unable to cope and William and Richard were packed off to the Grammar School in Hawkshead, a small stone or slate built village, quaint and picturesque in a hard kind of way in the Vale of Esthwaite. William was only eight or nine when he went there and he was allowed to be pretty wild and free: skating, climbing, flying kites, scrambling about in hazel trees gathering nuts, snaring, (poaching), swimming, boating, horseback riding (galloping along the sands of the Leven at midnight, and by moonlight.) From there, though, he went to a school in Penrith. He was now less free and therefore less happy – he admitted to an "over-love of freedom." It was here he met Mary Hutchinson, his future wife.

From there he went, even more unhappily, to St John's College, Cambridge, where he was like a bird "ill-tutored for captivity." "I was detached internally from academic cares," he explained. All the same he holidayed in Yorkshire, France and Switzerland. He graduated with a poor degree and drifted for four years. In London he heard Burke speak in the House of Commons, saw Mrs Siddons on stage, and watched the city crowds. Poetry, he was to say later, is "emotion recollected in tranquillity." In 1806 he recollected, in tranquillity, the stillness of London in the small hours:

> The river glideth at his own sweet will:
> Dear God! the very houses seem asleep;
> And all that mighty heart is lying still!

Then he crossed to France late in 1791 and stayed there for most of '92, the year which saw the end of the monarchy, the rise of the Republic, and the September Massacres. He became a Republican himself and met, and slept with, Annette Vallon; they had a daughter, Caroline. His money ran out as he was about to join the Girondins. Instead he caught the ferry to Dover. (His lover and daughter featured in his life only once more, when the Peace of Amiens let him visit France again. Caroline was then nine or ten.)

He turned to Godwinism, lured again perhaps by its

promise of freedom. Godwin was a kind of pre-Foucault anarchist; human passions, the rule of law, private property, marriage – all these things were oppressive. They had to go. (The Godwinian Revolution also planned to ban orchestras: something, perhaps, to do with oppressively forcing people to play notes in sequence?) Reason alone would free people from all illness and make them immortal. Wordsworth was taken in only briefly – a legacy of nine hundred pounds may have reconciled him to the rule of law and he retired with his sister, and the money, to Racedown in Dorset and, then in 1797 to the Quantock Hills in Somerset to be near Coleridge – a fellow mystic – and his family in Nether Stowey. (Cottle, the Bristol publisher, had introduced them.) There they were "three persons with one soul."

The Wordsworths rented a small mansion called Alfoxden House near Holford at the north-western end of the range. Dorothy said the area had everything. It still has: 'the wild simplicity' of the smooth summits – a thousand feet pressed against the sky, with Exmoor dropping in the blue distance into the sea. Below the crests of the hills are steep combes (wet, deep, green,) delicate with moss, dense with woods of slender trees, and flowing with stony brooks like the becks back home in Cumberland.

Hazlitt described Wordsworth the following year, 1798. He wore striped pantaloons and a fustian jacket (quaint even then). He was a tall, gaunt, lanky man who walked with a sailor-like gait and talked with a North Country accent (also provable from internal evidence: he once wrote 'note' as 'naught' and rhymed it with 'thought'). Hazlitt described the Roman-nosed face, familiar from his portraits, but adds something the painters missed: the 'convulsive inclination to laughter about the mouth'. More perceptively he remarked on " a fire in his eye (as if he saw something in objects more than the outward appearance)". Physically, and in time emotionally, Wordsworth and Coleridge were chalk and cheese. Coleridge self-described himself in a letter to Thelwall, the radical revolutionary: "My face, unless when animated by immediate eloquence, expresses great Sloth, &

great, indeed almost ideotic, good nature. 'Tis a mere carcase of a face: fat, flabby, & expressive chiefly of inexpression." "I cannot breathe thro' my nose," he added, "so my mouth, with sensual thick lips, is almost always open."

But there, in west Somerset, in the Quantock Hills and by the sea, Coleridge and Wordsworth between them changed English poetry when, in 1798, they brought out *Lyrical Ballads*. It introduced Romanticism to England, with a new kind of poetry – personal and emotional, in freer language – not dry, distant, classical and orderly like the verse of the passing Age of Reason. Wordsworth also wrote the famous Preface explaining that the new diction of their poetry was based on ballads and 'the real language of men', or rather (as somebody pointed out) the real 'written-prose language' of men. Wordsworth wrote about country people, Coleridge covered the Supernatural. Wordsworth was twenty-eight, Coleridge twenty-six.

All three of them, Coleridge, Wordsworth and Dorothy, spent the winter of 1798/9 in Germany. Coleridge became a Kantian; the idea that people see only what their brains allow them to, and that true reality might, therefore, be something very different, is an appealing thought for mystics. Wordsworth was just cold and homesick but he did begin the poem which, fifty years later, was published as *The Prelude*. In 1799 he and Dorothy settled in Grasmere where they lived for the rest of their lives, apart from walking tours and holidays. In 1802 Wordsworth married Mary Hutchinson. They had five children, only two of whom – the youngest and the oldest – outlived their parents. A boy and a girl, aged six and four, died in the same year (1812).

Socially it was a rich life. Grasmere, Ambleside and Derwentwater (where Ruskin had his first mystic experience aged all of four) are scenically lovely places. Many rich, famous or distinguished people visited or had second homes there. The Arnolds, for example, had a summer house – partly designed by Wordsworth – at Fox How. Dr Arnold, headmaster of Rugby, was a particular friend: Wordsworth complained he saw little of him because of the swarms of children. One of the swarm was Dr Arnold's son, Matthew, irredeemably unmystical, who later wrote *Dover Beach*, the poem which caught the sorrow the Victorians felt as Christianity failed.

As he aged and lost his mysticism, Wordsworth turned to Anglicanism, christianising some of his early and more pagan poetry. And yet he was never of the mechanical clockmaker school of believers. One wild morning he was talking to his four year old son about God, because the boy was asking questions. God is not like flesh, his father told him; more like a thought in your head. "There's a bit of him," he boy cried out, pointing through the window at the wind in the firs. His father, at four, would have agreed.

You can only do one thing well, he said, and for him that was poetry. He wrote a lot – far too much (seventy thousand lines; a record?) to be read comfortably – and from his late thirties he was a technically skilled worker in verse without the inspiration he once had. Sometimes he even reverted to the crusty diction of the Augustans.

He lived until 1850, nearly eighty, but Dorothy had begun to lose her mind when she was still only fifty-eight. His remaining daughter, Dora, had married and left home at thirty-seven; worse, she too died six years later. At seventy-three Wordsworth had been made Poet Laureate. Dorothy died in 1855, five years after her brother. Mary, wife and widow, survived them all.

Politically, he'd been a short-lived revolutionary, then a Radical who moved, as he matured, towards a kind of radical Toryism. Mystics, who sense the unchanging, are hardly likely to want to smash and start again, while people like him who sense "a pure principle of love" in the world tend to be humanitarian. Industrialism's warping effect on people upset him, as did the sheer ugliness it spawned. He was against building a railway to Windermere and proposed that the Lake District become – what it later did – a National Park. If he has to be labelled, 'Burkean' might suit. Burke was a Whig, of course, and Wordsworth a Tory – but both stood for liberty based on stability, continuity, and compassion.

Most people, he thought, are mystically inclined – except they're like illiterates with a book: they can't read what's written in the nature of things. It might be fairer to say some people are literate but misread the book, mistaking their experiences for something else. Others – a majority? – have no mystical leanings at all. They really are mystically illiterate. R S Thomas was one. He was, by all accounts, a strange old man, bitter and hate-ridden, but also a professional Christian, an Anglican priest, who spent his life searching for the God whose word he preached. He edited a book of Wordsworth's verse, and wrote the Introduction, without ever once realising that he was reading about the God he looked for.

FIFTEEN

The Thinking Mystic's Mariner

Samuel Taylor Coleridge (1772-1834) was a mystic (a mild one), a thinker (not a very good one), and an introvert (possibly a deep one). Not a world changing mix, you'd imagine, yet Mill called him one of the "seminal minds of his generation" and Wordsworth said he was the author of a whole string of "grand central truths". With Wordsworth he boosted – launched, even – the Romantic Movement in England. He helped to temper English Empiricism. Was at the bottom of American Transcendentalism. Influenced Christian Socialism. Modernised literary criticism. Rehabilitated *Hamlet*. Altered the way Shakespeare was staged (though he stole some ideas from Schelling.) His concept of Culture was picked up by Cardinal Newman, a fellow-mystic, and taken further by Arnold whose idea of the well-stocked mind was received wisdom in England until the 1960s, and still is for some older people.

Introverts of his thinking kind tend to be unstable, in turmoil, agitated, easily deflected, full of doubts – self-doubts and doubts about what they should think or do – and over-sensitive. Coleridge was all of these. A loneliness too deep for ending (in spite of friendships for which Coleridge had a genius) is a by-product. A stanza in *The Rime of the Ancient Mariner* says it all:

> O Wedding-guest! this soul hath been
> Alone on a wide wide sea:
> So lonely 'twas, that God himself
> Scarce seemèd there to be.

In the gloss alongside the verse he added: "In his loneliness and fixedness he yearneth towards the journeying Moon, and the stars that still sojourn, yet still move onward; and every where the blue sky belongs to them, and is their appointed rest, and their native country and their own natural homes."

People like him often need a shelter from the outer world – without it they're as lost as King Lear in the storm. That shelter can be drink, drugs, sex, or obsessions of any kind; in Coleridge's case it was laudanum – opium and brandy mixed and drunk by the pint. Best of all, however, is an overview or philosophy to explain how the world works, a way to account for the sheer oddity of Being, the strangeness of people. Thinking introverts like Coleridge are therefore also often system-builders, collecting ideas, cramming their minds with knowledge, gathering the raw material for a philosophy. One-sidedness – simple single-strand answers to complex questions – is rarely enough.

He seems to have instinctively seen things as binary systems: Reason and Understanding, Imagination and Fancy, Culture and Civilisation, Symbols and Allegories, each underpinned by mysticism. (Like Wordsworth, he thought the mystic experience was available to everybody because everything is interconnected. Each lesser mind can speak to the Greater Mind which is the underlying source of all being. When contact's made, the outcome is joy.)

Kant appealed to him because he set people free to believe in the supernatural, and Coleridge wanted to. Empiricism says you can only know what comes in through the eyes and ears. Nothing above nature – the super-natural – is therefore knowable. Kant pointed out that eyes, ears, and the brain they serve are made out of the same matter as the cosmos and so by definition can't see beyond it. A true reality could therefore exist although usually out of reach – except perhaps at times through beauty, presumably in flashes of mystic seeing.

Kant also gave him the concepts of Reason and Understanding, though what Coleridge meant by them are not what we mean today. 'Understanding' we'd now call reason or reasoning. By 'Reason' Coleridge seems to have meant mystic seeing, or what happens when thinking stops. It's the familiar dichotomy – intellect versus the mystic's eye which sees the spiritual. His prose is never all that clear but you can see exactly what he meant by 'Reason' in a stanza tacked on to the end of a prose essay *On the Constitution of Church and State*:

Whene'er the mist, that stands 'twixt God and thee,
Sublimates to a pure transparency,
That intercepts no light and adds no stain -
There Reason is, and then begins her reign !"

Imagination and Fancy went together in a binary way as well. Fancy is little more than memory – it recalls what's already been created but can't break it down to make something new. Imagination has already been touched on: it boils down to little more than one unprovable statement and one statement of the obvious. Imagination is creativity: God's creativity is at the higher level (unprovable), human creativity is at the lower. People make the world they live in by having access to God's creativity. Artists then use human creativity to break this God-and-Man made world down and re-use the bits in a work of art, a lesser creation.

But then, it follows logically, Creativity needs something to work on and that can only come from what's in the mind. The mind, therefore, has to be stocked high with knowledge. Adding knowledge broadens and deepens consciousness until, for the mystically inclined, a sub-mysticism of sorts is reached. Schools are one way to fill the mind, but who should in be charge? The churches? The State? Neither. Schools should be run by the Clerisy, a word Coleridge coined; it means the learned guardians and expanders of culture – scholars, scientists, writers, priests, philosophers. (Arnold, and others, used the word well into the 19th century but it's obsolete now: what it described has gone.)

By Civilisation Coleridge meant a society's physical infrastructure – roads, sewers, buildings (but not what happens inside). Today's Civilisation, in that case, would also include cars and computers. Civilisation is the hardware: Culture is the spiritual software resting on it. But without the spiritual there can be no liberty, no fully human people. The Clerisy's job is draw out inborn divinity.

A Coleridgean Symbol is whatever stops thought or shuts down the mind to let Eternity semi-shine translucently through. One evening in Malta he noticed the "moon dim-glimmering thro' the dewy window-pane". It was trying, he believed, to open up a way for the Eternity which was always hidden inside him to break surface and become consciously known.

Allegory meant what it still does – one thing standing for another. *The Pilgrim's Progress* is an allegory: Vanity Fair, the Slough of Despond, Doubting Castle, stand for states of mind or the vanities of the world. That, perhaps, is unfair to Bunyan; to some Pilgrim's story could be a Symbol allowing the Celestial City to shine through.

Coleridge's was a life of two halves with half-time coming at the age of forty-four. The first half was turbulent, hurt, drugged, baffled. The second was less drugged but infinitely more tranquil. The highlights – or lows – are often quoted. He tried to kill his brother with a knife over a bit of toasted cheese when they were boys in Ottery St Mary, their father's parish in Devon. As a Blue Coat Boy at Christ's Hospital he swam or waded fully clothed in the New River in north London and fell ill with jaundice and rheumatic fever (he's still of interest to medical historians because he was a life-long note-keeping hypochondriac given to quack remedies).

He ran away from Cambridge to join the 15th Light Dragoons though he couldn't sit a horse. Jesus College took him back after his brothers bought him out of the Army, pleading insanity. He left Cambridge without a degree. Already he was writing – sonnets for the London papers, to begin with. (After that he never stopped writing or lecturing or talking for the rest of his life: letters, reviews, articles, complete magazines, poetry, lectures, and a book – *Biographia Literaria*. Even the monologues of his old age were published as *Table Talk*.) With Southey he planned a Utopia in Pennsylvania to make people perfect by removing temptation. It came to nothing but he'd already married unhappily on the strength of it before it failed. Friends were already helping him: he had an annuity from the Wedgwood brothers until the war ruined them. Tom Poole let him have house next to his tannery in Nether Stowey. Cottle, the Bristol publisher, introduced him to the Wordsworths and there followed two revolutionary years in the Quantock Hills with them.

After nearly a year in Germany, he took is wife and family to live on the shores of Derwentwater to be near the Wordsworths in Westmorland. He fell in love with Mrs Wordsworth's sister, Sara Hutchinson. It was unreturned. He took time off to sail to Malta in a wartime military convoy to find himself. He didn't. Back in the Lake District he wrote, edited, and paid for another failed magazine, *The Friend*, with Sara's help. That was before the final split with the Wordsworths (they called him 'a rotten drunkard' behind his back). A spiral down into drugged and drunken despair ended in a suicidal nervous breakdown, in Bath of all genteel places (he was lecturing there). (Lesser mysticism doesn't always make for long term happiness, is one of the lessons of all this.)

Out of all this chaos he left two legacies: the importance of the well-stocked mind and *The Rime of the Ancient Mariner*. *The Ancient Mariner* is one of the greatest undertone-inducing poems in English as well as being Coleridge's greatest work – written when he was only twenty-five or six and never bettered. The poetry is good enough in places to be a thought-stopper, thus opening an avenue to the divine. An old lean sunburnt sailor stops a wedding guest and tells his strange tale about how, long ago, his ship had been driven into the south polar ice and trapped. An albatross led them to open water and, for no reason at all, the Mariner killed it with a cross-bow. In revenge the Polar Spirit drove the ship into the tropical Pacific and left her becalmed in rising heat. A ghostly ship came alongside. On board, Death and Life-in-Death diced for their souls. Death won the crew, Life-in-Death the Mariner, who was then left alive and alone with the dead.

> The very deep did rot: O Christ!
> That this should ever be!
> Yea, slimy things did crawl with legs
> Upon the slimy sea.

Nothing else lived. At first the Mariner despised these "creatures of the calm'. Then their beauty and happiness caused him to bless them, and the spell broke. It rained. He slept.

Angels raised the corpses of the crew to man the ship although it was really the spirit of the ice which drove her north to her home bay. There the angel-spirits appeared as they really are – seraphs of light. A pilot, his boy, and a holy hermit put out in a rowing boat to meet the ship. She split in two with a terrible crack and sank. The boy lost his mind, the pilot fainted, the hermit prayed, and the Mariner is compelled to travel (for ever more?) telling his tale to chosen listeners. His job is to "teach by his own example, love and reverence to all things that God made and loveth". This is from the marginalia, or gloss, which Coleridge added in 1817: you'd never guess it from the verse itself which merely tells us that the wedding guest arose 'the morrow morn a sadder and a wiser man'.

People have been trying to make head or tail of *The Ancient Mariner* ever since it was published in *Lyrical Ballads* in 1798. It was the lead poem until Wordsworth pulled it, saying it put readers off the rest of the book. Some took it allegorically; in a Ken Russell film of the 1970s, the albatross stands for Mrs Coleridge – literally: before your very eyes the bird changes into a woman clinging to his neck, the Pacific Ocean becomes Derwentwater, the doomed ship a rowing boat. Others say the bird stands for Dorothy Wordsworth or Sara Hutchinson (did Coleridge even *know* Sara when the poem was written?). Some read it as a morality tale about drug addiction. Others say it's about sin – against Nature or God, depending on taste. A lady complained the story had no moral. Coleridge corrected her; he regretted how bald its moral was. He meant the lines:

He prayeth best who loveth best,
All things both great and small:
For the dear God, who loveth us,
He made and loveth all.

Others think the Mariner was punished for violating the nature of things; love is the saving grace which offers him a half-redemption. This is the standard semi-mystic way to salvation – through love and a stopping of thought caused by beauty, in this case the beauty of the sea creatures seen for the first time, and properly, for what they are. For this reason it could have become a parable for semi-mystics – except for what happened to the Mariner afterwards.

The Ancient Mariner was mapped out in full one dark November evening in 1797 on an eight mile walk from Alfoxden, the semi-stately home the Wordsworths rented. Wordsworth suggested the albatross and the Polar Spirit but the poem was mainly put together from bits and pieces of reading. The mariner and wedding guest could be from Schiller's *Der Geisterseher*. Coleridge had already thought of writing a story about the Wandering Jew, with a not dissimilar plot of eternal wandering. Details of the ice and the torrid zone could be read in any of several 17th and 18th century books about sea voyages. The killing of an albatross is probably from Shelvocke's *Voyage Round the World* (1726); the captain shot the great bird because he thought it was an ill omen causing the storms which are endemic in the Roaring Forties. Coleridge himself seemed more interested in writing something for cash – he hoped Cottle, the Bristol publisher, would give him five pounds for *The Ancient Mariner* (a lot of money; at the time he was getting an annuity from the Wedgwoods, the pottery people, of just under three pounds a week). In other words, the poem had no thought-through coherent theme, not a conscious one at any rate. It works, not because of the story, but through images, colour, and resonance. It's flat and apparently depthless, un-rounded, easily and quickly read, and very brightly coloured.

It's a simplicity of ice and cold, fog and snow, without the pain. It's a simplicity too of heat and the skin-scouring salt of the sea. A blood-red sun rises, curves in a parabola across a copper coloured sky, and sets in an unmoving ocean. In all this dew-less heat the flat sea is the colour of winter frost, while in the shadow of the hull the water burns an 'awful' red.

In it swim water snakes – 'blue, glassy green, and velvet black' whose tracks flash with a 'golden fire'. Even the northern bay is bright with white moonlight and crimson shadows, while the seraph-men shine with their own light. Silence often prevails too. The weathervane on the steeple is 'steeped in silentness'. These things enter the soul and stay there – as well as being a source of word-mysticism quite good enough to put a stopper on thought.

The simplicity of the prosody helps. It's in ballad form – mainly quatrains of which the second and fourth lines have six syllables (more or less), while the other two have eight (more or less). Each stanza always has four rhymes but not always *abab* – some are internal to a single line.

> The sun came up upon the left,
> Out of the sea came he!
> And he shone bright, and on the right
> Went down into the sea.

Occasionally quatrains give way to six line stanzas with internal rhyme:

> And I had done a hellish thing,
> And it would work 'em woe :
> For all averred, I had killed the bird
> That made the breeze to blow.
> Ah wretch! said they, the bird to slay,
> That made the breeze to blow!

After his breakdown, friends took Coleridge to Calne in Wiltshire to recover. He collected and edited his poetry under the title *Sibylline Leaves*. It was the year of Waterloo, 1815. In four months he drafted out his *Biographia Literaria*, one of the great texts of Romanticism. It rambles a bit, with chapters of anecdotes, but also lays out the ideas he set such great store by – Imagination (or Esemplastic Power) in particular. He covers prosody, Wordsworth's poetry, the Preface to *Lyrical Ballads*, Associationism from Aristotle to Hartley, a criticism of Shakespeare's *Venus and Adonis*, and much more.

He was forty-four, with just under twenty years to live. A Dr Gillman and his wife took him to live with them in Highgate on the northern hills above London. His opium habit eased off but he never broke it entirely. He died peacefully of a heart attack in the summer of 1834.

Carlyle used to take a carriage up into the hills on visits. He called the hills a place of groves and villas, "a waving blooming country of the brightest green." London in the valley below was seen through an 'olive-tinted haze.' Coleridge's room was upstairs at the back with the best view of the garden, and the gardens of other tree-hidden houses. "The good man," Carlyle wrote, "he was now getting old, towards sixty perhaps; and gave you the idea of a life that had been full of sufferings; a life heavy-laden, half-vanquished, still swimming painfully in seas of manifold physical and other bewilderment. ... The deep eyes, of a light hazel, were as full of sorrow as of inspiration; confused pain looked mildly from them, as in a kind of mild astonishment." In his last years, said Lamb, Coleridge "had a hunger for Eternity."

His house in The Grove is still there – a three-storey red brick building on a triangle of green and an avenue of limes – just across the road from The Flask, an early 18th century inn where they say Hogarth drank his ale. Coleridge's extension stands proud of the older part of the house. It has a mansard roof of red tiles and a dormer window. (J B Priestley lived there for a while.) Kenwood House, a stately 18th century mansion, is a near neighbour. In its grounds you can still get the flavour of those hills of groves and villas that Carlyle wrote about; it's above a deep valley, with several small streams or rills and artificial lakes (one's called The Thousand Pound Pond – what it cost to dig it out). The hills are sand on clay; ponds, springs, wells, and small rills are everywhere. It was a good place for Coleridge to be: sheltered, in the country, but from where he could drop down within an hour into one of the world's great cities to lecture and talk.

Six years after he died the Highgate Literary and Scientific Institution opened on Pond Square close to his house in The Grove. What would he have made of that?

SIXTEEN

The Cardinal and the Clerisy

John Henry Newman (1801-1890) fits Coleridge's description of the clerisy pretty well – a defender and expander of culture, although in the long run that same culture turned out to be undefendable: within seventy or eighty years of his death it too was almost dead. Still, for some, he remains an expander in the rubble. Coleridge was twenty-nine when Newman was born: *The Rime of the Ancient Mariner* was behind him, his mature ideas still ahead. He'd been dead for seventeen years when Newman became Rector of the new Catholic University in Dublin, in 1851. His ideas on the other hand lived on in Newman's head, and the bishops didn't like them. They wanted their university to turn out people groomed for the guinea-earning professions. The outcome of the stand-off was a book, *The Idea of a University* (1852) in which Coleridge's ideas are expanded.

Like everybody else Newman was hampered by a lack of words for what he wanted to say. What is the chief characteristic of a properly functioning healthy intellect? "Illumination," was Newman's best shot: the intellect should shine with an inner light – it should be lit, illuminated, luminous. Luminosity comes when the intellect has over-all understanding or overview of its own civilisation – its history, philosophy, literature, art. "We perfect our nature, not by undoing it, but by adding to it what is more than nature, and directing it towards aims higher than its own." Matthew Arnold, a follower of Newman, put it even better a few years later: the well-lit intellect is what results from "knowing the best of what's been thought and said."

Creating a well-lit intellect is a university's job. Other studies – geology or law, for example – could be tacked on later. Culture first, quartz and torts next. The well-filled mind, moreover, is a good thing in its own right. "Nothing is excellent, beautiful, perfect, desirable for its own sake, but it overflows, and spreads a likeness of itself all around it." "A great good will impart a great good." "A good mind ... is a good to all around it." "The cultivated intellect brings with it a power and grace to every work."

Having said that, people also need the spiritual because the intellect, however cultivated, can't on its own avoid "passion and pride". To reach entelechy – to be properly evolved and developed, rounded and fulfilled – you need both philosophy and religion. They go together because deep down the intellect and the spiritual are the same, a mystic's view of the oneness underlying disparity, unity below diversity.

Nature, in fact, *requires* a well-stocked mind: it's partly what it's for. But there's more to it than that – a well-filled mind sees things beyond the reach of the senses. And here, again, there's no word for what he wanted to say: he settled for a phrase – 'implicit reasoning'. If the hidden, lower, unconscious mind is left alone with its store of knowledge, it will generate ideas which are better than anything conscious thought can come up with. Reason is then called in to test them. Do they work? If they do, then they are, in some way, true. (He was a Pragmatist before Pragmatism was invented.) This also applies to mild mysticism: if it works then it, too is a kind of truth.

Put it all together and you get, or so he believed, a gentleman (presumably a 21st century Newman would include women?). A gentleman will have "a cultivated intellect, a delicate taste, a candid, equitably dispassionate mind, a noble and courteous bearing in the conduct of life." "A habit of mind is formed which lasts through life, of which the attributes are, freedom, equitableness, calmness, moderation, and wisdom."

Cardinal John Henry Newman was a mystic, albeit a closet or covert one. He said of himself when he was a child: "I thought life might be a dream or I an angel, and all this world a deception." At fifteen he became a Calvinist, certain of salvation. This didn't make him careless of God, he explained in *Apologia Pro Vita Sua* – just isolated from the world and doubtful of its reality. Two things only were "absolute and luminously self-evident, myself and my Creator." Later, as an Church of England vicar, he preached: "What we see is but the outward shell of an eternal kingdom." The visible world is the veil of the invisible. It 'conceals and yet suggests' things beyond itself which have neither shape nor are made of matter. In any religion, he thought, there'll always be the exoteric and the esoteric. He was on the side of the latter. Like many mystics he was (in all probability) an introvert – what else can 'isolated from the world and doubtful of its reality' mean?

His father had been a banker (part-owner of his own bank, that is) until the peace at the end of the Napoleonic Wars ruined him. He then went down to Hampshire to manage a brewery in Alton before (perhaps) running a pub in Clerkenwell. His eldest son, John Henry, was good at maths, played the violin (later composed a violin concerto), was not a great Classicist, but liked reason and reasoning.

He was ready for university at sixteen, but which one? A post chaise was kept waiting outside the front door while his father and mother made up their minds. The curate of St James's in Piccadilly pitched in and suggested Oxford, which is where the boy went and from there into history. (A good story which deserves to be true even if it isn't.) A scholarship worth £540 over nine years kept him in Oxford but poor marks in Trinity put paid to a career in the law. Instead he became, more congenially, a Fellow of Oriel, *the* intellectual college of its day. He stayed for twenty years. He was ordained at twenty-three and given the living of the university church of St Mary's six years later. Undergraduates crowded in to hear his preaching. Matthew Arnold wrote: "who can forget the charm of that spiritual apparition, gliding through the dim afternoon light of St Mary's, rising into the pulpit and then breaking the silence with a spiritual music, subtle, sweet, mournful?"

In 1832-3, in his own early thirties, he set off on on a tour of the Mediterranean with his friend Hurrel Froude and Froude's father. They sailed to Gibraltar, Malta, Ionia, then back to Naples, Rome and Sicily where he fell ill with typhoid fever. His recovery led him to believe God had work for him. On the voyage home, becalmed for a week in the strait between Corsica and Sardinia, he wrote the hymn, *Lead Kindly Light*, which sounds quintessentially Victorian though William IV was still on the throne. It sums up one of Newman's core beliefs: God eventually guides everybody home.

> Lead, kindly Light, amid th'encircling gloom, lead
>   Thou me on!
> The night is dark, and I am far from home; lead Thou
>   me on!
> Keep Thou my feet; I do not ask to see
> The distant scene; one step is enough for me.

That summer in England (1833) saw the beginning of the Oxford or Tractarian Movement. Newman himself said it began with one of John Keble's sermons speaking out against Parliamentary meddling in the church (ten Anglican Sees in Ireland had been cut). That Autumn Newman wrote the first of the Tracts (hence the name Tractarian). Pusey joined the three co-founders – Keble, Froude, and Newman – a year or so later. Their job, as they saw it, was to define and defend the Church of England – re-rooting it in its pre-Reformation past, making it plain that it was not only the middle way between Catholic and Protestant but was also in unbroken direct descent from the Apostles. What exactly was the Elizabethan Settlement? was the kind of question they asked. What does consecration mean when applied to the Eucharist? Does baptism change the soul? Newman's sermons reinforced his Tracts. The direction for some (such as Pusey) was towards Anglo-Catholicism, for others (such as Newman) towards undiluted Catholicism. In Tract 90, the last of them all, Newman argued that the Thirty-Nine Articles didn't exclude Catholicism; even the doctrine of Purgatory could be fitted in. The uproar ended his career as an Anglican vicar. He was forty-two.

He went to Littlemore, then a village outside Oxford (now a suburb inside it) where he stayed in a single storey stone building, called the College, enclosing a quad or garden. Here he wrote *The Development of Christian Doctrine*. All things change ("to be perfect is to have changed often"). The church also changes, but why? By what authority? The Bible's unchanging, so it can't be Scripture. In any case on its own the Bible isn't enough – Protestants misuse it in making it the answer to everything. Unheretical change, he concluded, can only come through an unbroken linkage to the Apostles, and therefore to Christ Himself. Change is then guided by the Holy Spirit – the Unchanging, that is, acting on the changeful in this brief stay of Creation. At Littlemore, too, he was received, aged forty-five, into the Catholic church by an Italian missionary, Dominic Barberi.

One of his first acts as a Catholic was to set up an Oratory in Birmingham based on the rule of St Philip Neri (1515-1595). Oratories are not unlike university common rooms or an officer's mess – un-monk-like secular monasteries whose priest-members pay for their meals (though probably not bar bills) out of their own money. They also own their own furniture and clothes, and can leave when they want. There's a minimum age of thirty-six, and no vows. It's a kind of democracy with one priest one vote. Even the Superior can be voted out of office, and in fact is voted in for only three years at a time. For an expelled Fellow of Oriel it was a home from home and Newman lived there for the best part of the next forty-five years.

Catholicism suited him in spite of the malice of some fellow Catholics who gave him so much trouble over the years – the Achili affair to begin with. Achili was a Dominican monk and rapist who'd taken to attacking the Church. Newman tried to discredit him with an *ad hominem* attack in a lecture in 1852. He thought it safe to do so because Cardinal Wiseman had already written about the man. Achili sued. Wiseman couldn't find the papers. A friend went to Italy to look for the women the monk had raped. Most of them (now married and with children) didn't want to testify, even in a foreign court. The jury found Newman guilty. His appeal was lost, though he was then fined (and lectured on his degeneracy by the judge) instead of jailed.

So much money had been collected, in the USA in particular, that enough was left over to pay, in part, for the church he had built in Dublin – Our Lady Seat of Wisdom – when he was appointed Rector of the new University. It's modelled on Byzantine basilica-like buildings in Ravenna. Where other converts like Cardinal Manning favoured the rococo Catholic south, Newman found it a bit overblown; he was reserved, English, and drawn to the quietness of the Desert Fathers, the simplicity of the mystic.

Then, in 1864, Charles Kingsley, in a review of Froude's *History of England*, effectively called Newman a liar: "truth for its own sake need not be ... a virtue of the Roman clergy." The result was *Apologia Pro Vita Sua* (a defence of his life) (1865). It's a spiritual autobiography, a Wordsworthian pilgrimage in prose, recording the evolving changes in his mind since childhood, but only touching on his mysticism, never dwelling on it. Kingsley's slur was particularly hard to take because Newman was a kind of ecclesiastical Darwinian; – everything evolves and changes. The church had. He did. A boy's truth is not a man's truth.

That same year, now aged sixty-four, he published his long poem, *The Dream of Gerontius*, about the progress of a soul from death to judgement. The poem opens with a priest imploring mercy until, abruptly, all lapses into a peacefulness in which Newman outlines (possibly, perhaps even probably) his own mystic experiences.

> I went to sleep; and now I am refresh'd,
> A strange refreshment: for I feel in me
> An inexpressive lightness, and a sense
> Of freedom, as I were at length myself,
> And ne'er had been before. How still it is!
> I hear no more the busy beat of time,
> No, nor my fluttering breath, nor struggling pulse;
> Nor does one moment differ from the next.

125

At first *Gerontius* thinks he's still in his body though he can't move, not even an eyelid, and is blind – yet he can hear and feel; he hears singing and feels himself lifted. It's the Angel-guardian who's steered him through life. Gerontius is now simply called Soul, no longer a man, nor old. Can he ask questions? Yes, the Angel tells him, nothing you want can now be wrong; whatever you do is right. When we die, Gerontius/Soul says, I thought we went straight to the Judgement Seat? Sun-time and clock-time no longer apply, he's told: only thought-time. The depth of your own thought is slowing you down. So why aren't I afraid? Soul/Gerontius asks. You were so afraid before you died that all the fear has been burned up. More than that, Judgement has already begun and you sense that all will eventually be well. (Everything in the immaterial world, by the way, is fully alive – even the paving stones and bricks are life itself.)

Will I see God? Soul asks. You're disembodied but, because that might be unbearable, you've been given what appear to be earthly senses, apart from sight. You'll be blind in the fires of Purgatory, which burn without light, but first, for a moment, you'll see the face of God. The sight will open a wound, and heal the wound, and widen the wound all at the same time. The sight of the Divine will make you sick with love but filled with shame for what you did wrong in life. Because, in effect, this is not so much a judgement as a revelation, the coming of understanding. Each soul will want to be punished because it's the right thing to do. (Dante has something similar; Arnaut Daniel, the troubadour, dives gladly back into the flame to be refined, like gold: "Remember my pain, I pray you, when you reach the summit of the stair".) Soul hears the priest on earth still intoning the last word of his prayer: "*subvenite*" – help. No earth time has passed at all.

Unsurprisingly, God is not described. Soul merely says: "Ah!..."

> Take me away, and in the lowest deep
> There let me be,
> And there in hope the lone night-watches keep.

For minor mystics *Gerontius* might be a bit overripe, overwrought, overblown and overdone, too distant from the experience of pure simplicity. *Gerontius* tried to be spiritual but doesn't succeed: *The Ancient Mariner* didn't, and does. Victorian schoolboys might have called it 'pi' – pious in a sickly kind of way. (This is true even if, in one passage, demons scoff at mortals for being "psalm-droners and canting groaners.") It worked for its time, however: mostly. General Gordon (1833-1885), terrified of the afterlife, had a copy sent to him in Egypt in 1884. He read it on his journey to his own death in Khartoum. This copy, with pencilled notes, was later given as a wedding present to Elgar. Elgar set it to music as an Oratorio, scoring the part of the Angel-guardian for a soprano voice. It was premiered (disastrously) at the 1900 Birmingham Festival and played again in 2008 to mark the re-opening of Symphony Hall in that same city. Newman had no great gift for the glittering line and Elgar's music lifts it only a little – it doesn't have that quiet mood of sadness needed to induce mildly mystic experiences. The message is a kind one – all will be well – yet that mystical sense of an underlying immaterial purity and simplicity is lost in a welter of overblown imagery.

But even as he wrote *Gerontius*, he knew religion was dying in an England sliding quietly into a God-free future. What could he give his Godless unborn countrymen? Not much, as it turned out. The nub of his book about the problem, *An Essay in Aid of a Grammar of Assent* (1870), is that people can believe without either understanding or proof. Understanding the mystery of it all is impossible. No proof of God's existence is possible either. Nothing can join the mind to the truth with the solidity of an iron bar: instead the reason for belief is like a rope made of thin fibres none of which alone is strong but, woven together, can support certainty. That certainty is then tested by reason. Given good quality evidence reason tends to get things right. It doesn't work of course and anyway it's all pretty pointless because in the end, as Newman said, only inner conviction convinces: *Cor ad Cor loquitur* (let heart speak to heart) was his motto. Agnosticism, in his opinion, is the only option for the mystically blind. But that, surely, applies to everyone?

SEVENTEEN

The Second Mystic Laureate

Lord Tennyson was a lifelong and a long lived mystic (he was born in 1809 and died in 1892). "I've often," he said, "had a strange feeling of being bound and wrapped in the Great Soul." He also admitted: "I get carried away out of sense and body, and rapt into mere existence." He knew, too, "the unreality of the material and the reality of the spiritual world." When he was doubted he cried: "by God Almighty, there is no delusion in the matter! It is no nebulous ecstasy, but a state of transcendent wonder, associated with absolute clearness of mind." He knew that 'freezing reason' froze the gateway shut, and that repeating a mantra (his own name) brought on the mystic experience which, in the end, is beyond understanding. Canto 124 of *In Memoriam* spells it all out. He begins by saying he doesn't know what the Eternal is – is it "He, They, One, All"? Proofs of God's existence are pushed aside, particularly the argument from design ("eagle's wing, or insects eye"), along with flimsy theologies spun from men's brains:

> I found Him not in world or sun,
> Or eagle's wing, or insect's eye;
> Nor thro' the questions men may try,
> The petty cobwebs we have spun:

But these are petty things which are by-passed by the mystical experience itself, when a ...

> ... warmth within the breast would melt
> The freezing reason's colder part,
> And like a man in wrath the heart
> Stood up and answer'd 'I have felt.'

Feel or felt – there's no proof, just a happening. At those times he was like a child, fearful and crying, but a child who also knew his father was close by, and so was safe. He can see but not understand what underlies all things:

> And what I am beheld again
> What is, and no man understands;
> And out of darkness came the hands
> That reach thro' nature, moulding men.

Why then, given all this, did he spend seventeen years writing *In Memoriam*, a long poem asking: 'what's it all about'? He started it as a twenty-four year old in 1833 and finished it aged forty-one in 1850 – from early adulthood to middle age. There are a hundred and thirty-one cantos or short elegies (plus a prologue and epilogue) and all to answer the question: is there life after death, a God who cares? The questions were raised by the death of Arthur Hallam, a friend from his Cambridge days who died suddenly in Vienna in September, 1833.

The range of the cantos is wide: Tennyson was well-read in the science of his day, and a convinced pre-Darwinian evolutionist. He describes despair, resignation, consolation – "'Tis better to have loved and lost/Than never to have loved at all." Words themselves are questioned – "I sometimes hold it half a sin/To put in words the grief I feel', except that words can be like drugs to numb the pain of the 'unquiet heart'. In another passage he feels he's physically merging with a thousand year old yew in a rural churchyard; the griefless tree stands unaltered and unaging while time changes everything around it and, century after century, the church clock strikes the hours.

He covers time, geology (the pre-Darwinian reason for belief in evolution) and other aspects of science. Some scientific materialism he doubted, but never evolution. At the end of the poem he looks ahead to a time when mankind will have evolved into a different species, one that's "no longer half-akin to brute". Before then, however, he worries about where we're all heading: whole species have come and gone – whither, therefore, a mankind who ...

... trusted God was love indeed
And love creation's final law -
Tho' Nature red in tooth and claw
With ravine, shrieked against his creed -

Who loved, who suffer'd countless ills,
Who battled for the True, the Just,
Be blown about the desert dust,
Or seal'd within the iron hills?

In Memoriam's turning point, a mystical one (although later thrown away), comes in Canto 95, nearly three-quarters of the way through. Tennyson had been sitting with his family and their friends all one summer afternoon on the lawn of his father's vicarage at Somersby in Lincolnshire. The whole scene is curiously Victorian – it could be in no other reign, except it was; William IV was still on the throne. (The year is thought to be either in 1836 or '37 when Tennyson was in his mid-twenties). Family, friends, guests sat late into the long warm evening talking, singing, drinking tea (an urn 'fluttered' on a table). The air was so still the candle flames never wavered, and they heard the brook in the distance. Bats flitted, white cattle glimmered in the late twilight. One by one, family and friends went to bed and the poet, now alone, re-read Hallam's letters. And all at once, the reassuring mystic experience came to him.

So word by word, and line by line,
The dead man touch'd me from the past,
And all at once it seem'd at last
The living soul was flash'd on mine,

And mine in this was wound, and whirl'd
About empyreal heights of thought,
And came on that which is, and caught
The deep pulsations of the world.

Doubt broke up what he called the 'trance' which must have lasted some hours since the dawn breeze was rising in the sycamores, and rocking the elms, the roses, and the lilies when it ended. The wind dropped and Western night and

Eastern morning began to "broaden into common day".

In 1878 Tennyson altered two of the above words. "The living soul' had been "His living soul" and "mine in this" had been 'mine in his." Why he changed them is unknown. Mystical union with a dead friend is unusual, if not unique, and smacks of hysteria rather than the real thing. Many people in Tennyson's own day thought his grief was a bit over-done and unmanly.

That should have been enough but, in spite of all this mysticism, the poem's ending could have been written by any fox-hunting curate, if he'd had a way with words.

> We have but faith: we cannot know;
> For knowledge is of things we see;
> And yet we trust it comes from thee,
> A beam in darkness: let it grow.

Agnosticism like is this the only honest thing to be but mysticism is a sensing of something deeper and this seems to be a bit of a cop out. Was he just giving the public what they wanted? It was certainly popular: the Queen herself, it's said, kept a copy by her bed along with the Bible. In the end, contradicting the doubting curate in himself, he believes Hallam now lives on with "That God ..

> ... which ever lives and loves,
> One God, one law, one element,
> And one far-off divine event,
> To which the whole creation moves.

He never moved mysticism any further along. What he did do, all his life, was write poetry good enough to blank out thought. Hallam was buried in the church on his family's estate at Clevedon by the Wye, a river which flows into the Severn. Up to this point, the Severn is tidal. Salt water from the sea at high tide dams the Wye and stops it flowing. In Canto 19, he compares his own grief (now lesser, now deeper) to the ebb and flow of the tide in the rivers. The outcome for the reader is word-mysticism – words which can stop thought – as well as undertones which are contained in the imagery of the sea and a river meeting below timbered hills:

> There twice a day the Severn fills;
> The salt sea-water passes by,
> And hushes half the babbling Wye,
> And makes a silence in the hills.

He was in his mid-seventies when he wrote *The Passing of Arthur*, the last idyll of *The Idylls of the King*. In it are lines powerful enough to be thought-stoppers, though there's nothing overtly mystical about the stories at all. The whole series is a re-working of the Matter of Britain, stories set around King Arthur, Camelot, and the Table Round, as told by Malory and the *Mabinogion*. They're mainly tales of betrayal. *The Passing of Arthur* tells of the last great battle in the West when "all day long the noise of battle roll'ed/Among the mountains by the winter sea." All the knights of the Round Table have been killed, save for Sir Bedivere, while the King himself is mortally wounded and carried by barge to the apple isle of Avalon ...

> Where falls not hail, or rain, or any snow,
> Nor ever wind blows loudly; but it lies
> Deep-meadowed, happy, fair with orchard lawns
> And bowery hollows crowned with summer sea.

Avalon isn't heaven, it's more of a waiting place from where the once-and-future king will return to save his country when it needs him. (How big must that need be, if he hasn't turned up yet?) It's an un-Christian and an unmystical ending. The Love and Hope of *In Memoriam* are abandoned here and all is bleak (warmth and sunshine are to be found only in the apple orchard isle of Avalon, out of reach of the living). But it does have the right mystic mood of sadness – tears for the passing away of greatness, the coming of the alien and lesser. God Himself has gone:

> "I found Him in the shining of the stars,
> I marked Him in the flowering of His fields,
> But in His ways with men I find Him not."

Sir Bedivere, the first and last of the Table Round, is left in the world alone:

"And I, the last, go forth companionless,
And the days darken round me, and the years,
Among new men, strange faces, other minds."

And slowly answered Arthur from the barge:
"The old order changeth, yielding place to new,
And God fulfils himself in many ways."

Once again Tennyson redeems himself through word-mysticism – thought stopping words to let the Ultimate come through. The sadness of defeat is also an undertone. Mysticism is implicit in these things, though probably unintentionally.

Crossing the Bar was written at the very end of Tennyson's life. He was eighty. "This crowns your life's work," a friend said. "Yes," Tennyson agreed, "it came to me in a moment." That moment, it seems, came in 1889 on the Isle of Wight ferry. He'd been very ill, in fact had only three years to live.

Sunset and evening star,
And one clear call for me!
And may there be no moaning of the bar,
When I put out to sea,

But such a tide as moving seems asleep,
Too full for sound and foam,
When that which drew from out the boundless deep
Turns again home.

Twilight and evening bell,
And after that the dark!
And may there be no sadness of farewell,
When I embark;

For tho' from out our bourne of Time and Place
The flood may bear me far,
I hope to see my Pilot face to face
When I have crost the bar.

"The Pilot has been on board all the while," he explained, "but in the dark I have not seen him." The poem's a mix of the conventionally Christian and the mystical (what came out of the boundless deep is now going home). Some of the lines are mild mind-shutters but even more powerful are the undertones: once heard – preferably in childhood – the imagery resonates for a lifetime.

And yet you can't help feeling let down by Tennyson. Most probably he was a mid-level mystic, and intermittent with it. Mystic episodes may have been the bones of his belief (such as it was, and it wasn't much), but building a body on bones hides them. What if the bones are more valuable than the body? The setting of Canto 19 (where the hushed Wye makes a silence in the hills) is close to Tintern Abbey where, nearly forty years before, Wordsworth wrote one of the best descriptions we have of the mystic state. Wordsworth was the greater mystic, Tennyson the better poet, which makes it even more of a pity he buried his mystical insights so deeply in his verse. Mystics with a flare for words at Tennyson's level are rare.

EIGHTEEN

Unthoroughfaresomeness

Most people think of Gerard Manley Hopkins (1844-1889) as a poet. First and foremost, though, he was a Catholic priest, a Jesuit. As a poet he was an original and an oddity, probably because he wrote largely in isolation: Coventry Patmore (a fellow mystic) and the Rev. Dixon, a canon in Carlisle Cathedral, read some of his work but only Robert Bridges knew it in full, and it was Bridges in fact who had his work published in 1917. A second batch came out in 1948, nearly a hundred years after his birth and sixty after his death.

Isolated writers, of course, aren't isolated readers and some of his ideas were borrowed. His poetry too, though more original than most, has a background – Shakespeare to begin with for word handling (compounding words to make new ones) and Milton for prosodic flexibility. Often, too, his work reminds people of Anglo-Saxon kennings – portmanteau words such, for example, as 'whale-road' for the sea or 'bone-house' for the body (a structure which he did in fact use). Yet, apparently, he didn't learn Old English until he was thirty-eight, and never did read Cynewulf or Beowulf. On the other the hand, an eccentric movement to de-Latinise, or re-Teutonise, English was launched around the time he was born. Also, the Early English Text Society was founded by Furnivall and Trench while he was still at Oxford. Trench had been lecturing and writing since Hopkins's childhood about how English might sound had it never been hybridised with Latin and Greek. *Impenetrability*, for example, could be *unthoroughfaresomeness*. So to penetrate to the heart of things, mystically speaking, could be *to thoroughfare*. This kind of penetrability could then be called *thoroughfaresomeness*. (There is a word, 'thoroughfare', of course – a route between two places – in fairly common use.)

If that's never going to catch on, what about *again-buying* for redemption, which is more reasonable since it lights up the meaning at bit more? *Fellowfeel*, too, is more trenchant than *sympathise* – and 'fellow feeling' is a phrase in fairly regular use. William Barnes (1801-1886), the Dorset dialect poet, invented many Hopkins-like replacements to replenish (re-fill?) the 'wordstore of the landfolk': *footkeys* for pedals, *gleecraft* for music, *outclear* for elucidate, *speechcraft* for grammar, *sleepstow* for dormitory, *sunprint* or *sunflame* for photograph (what would television be? *Farsunflame*? *Farsight*?). Hopkins-like coinages (and his include shadowtackle, hardy-handsome, flake-doves) were in the Victorian air. These words themselves have undertones of what might have been. Can you have nostalgia for what never was – rather than for what is no more?

Less usually, for an English-speaking writer, he was influenced by Welsh. He learned the language well enough to read poetry in it and write one or two poems himself. *Cynghanedd* (pronounced something like kung – han -eth) is the generic noun for intricate rules of prosody and patterns of consonance, assonance, alliteration, as well as internal rhymes and half-rhymes. This is Hopkins's successful attempt at *cynghanedd lusg*:

O is he dead th*en*? My duty all *en*ded?

Here he doesn't quite pull of cynghanedd draws:

worm-laid grave (of a) womb-life grey.

The w, l, and g alliterate but laid and life should share a final consonant, and don't. Prosody is also starting to take precedence over sense.

His best shot at *cynghanedd sain* is:

The down-dugged ground-hugged grey

with its internal rhyme and fairly correct (we're told) alliteration and consonance.

What he's best known for – Sprung Rhythm – wasn't really his at all: it's the age-old way of writing verse in English. Probably it's as old as the language, being the staple meter of

Beowulf, the Border Ballads, and Little Bo-Peep. You count the stressed syllables, ignore the unstressed. That's the essence: everything else is an add-on, such as 'outrides' (unheeded extra syllables; a way of outwitting the rules) and 'over-reaving' (the stanza, not the line, is the basic unit). By sprung he meant abrupt (because the words jump). His poems have little slackness, only highly stressed tension – Coiled Spring Rhythm, perhaps. Out of it came a tough, sinewy, punchy, flexible poetry in which words work like drills and detonators.

More originally, in a letter written one midnight to a friend, he sketched in a way of categorising poetry. He divided it into four: Delphic – not far above daily prose; Parnassian – workmanlike but open to imitation; Castalian – peculiar to a single mind but still in its journeyman mode, although more inspired. The highest kind he left unnamed except to call it 'poetry proper'. Most of the best poetry is Castalian with sudden unexpected lines of 'poetry proper' (Shakespeare is full of it, nobody better). Poetry proper is a gift, something given, and can't be written at will. Nobody can force it. Nevertheless, this is what Hopkins opted for, trying to by-pass the Parnassian and Castalian and make every line alive with poetry proper – "loading every rift with ore," as Keats put it.

His ideas to explain the mystic insight are, naturally enough, his own although even here he liked to be buttressed by other people. In his early years he was very 'Ruskinese', as he called it; his note books are full of minute details of nature, both written and sketched, as decreed by Ruskin. Beauty, Ruskin believed, arises from the right combination of symmetry and variety – in a leaf, flower, tree, cloud or whatever. Probably this was Ruskin's way of making sense of his own experiences of what is beyond the physical. Two things are involved: what changes and what is changeless. What changes (variety) overlays what is unchanging (symmetry): unstillness on stillness; changing things flickering over the unchanging, unity underlying diversity. 137

But Hopkins had the same mystic experiences as Ruskin.

To partly explain them, he invented two words: *inscape* and *instress*. Inscape is the particularity of things, their unique shape or being, the thing that makes them what they are and different from everything else. All oak leaves are vaguely alike – they have a common template – yet each is also uniquely different because of inscape. But inscape is also what triggers mental shut-down to let the small time mystic catch a brief sight of the great unchanging basis of all creation. What connects the mind to this Beyondness is a force Hopkins called instress. Instress also holds the inscape together in its unique guise. Each inscape, to put it another way, is like a uniquely shaped window opening onto a mystic garden; instress is the energy holding the window together, but it's also the energy of the sunlight which both lets you to see the garden, and also keeps it in being, growing and flowering. This energy is God's. Everything you see, therefore, is shot through with God's power, and God is therefore discernible through everything – everything beautiful, that is.

As a young Jesuit novice he was a bit distrustful of such ideas. Were they orthodox? He was twenty-four when he coined these two words: four years later he read Duns Scotus on haecceity (or thisness) and felt justified; Scotus, after all, was a doctor of the Church who'd probably taught in Oxford (around 1300) and was a defender of the Immaculate Conception, which appealed to Hopkins, a devout Marian. Scholars now say that Scotist haecceity and Aquinan quiddity (whatness) are, apparently, not quite what Hopkins thought they were, but never mind, he had his authority. Ever after he always thought of Scotus when he found himself in a rustic landscape.

Inscape, or thisness, or self, was essential to Hopkins. A thing broken is a thing un-selfed (unselved); the pattern, which made it what was, has gone. Inscape is self-ness. (In-self, it could be better called.) This is not self-centredness. Scotist thisness and Ignatian self-denial come together. Self-denial leads to the flowering of self as it was meant to be. In God's eyes, Hopkins believed, such a person is Christ Himself. The self is near perfection when it simply is, without selfishness or self-obsession. Selfishness unselves people.

Inscape, incidentally, has an antonym – scaping. A poor work of art can be said to have scaping: its instress has collapsed leaving it shapeless and flaccid. Self-absorbed people (presumably) also have scapings since they're less than they could be, deflated by escaping energy.

More usefully, because they describe something demonstrably real, Hopkins also coined *underthought* and *overthought*. Overthought is what people normally mean by thought – what a thinker is overtly thinking and saying. Underthoughts are often unconsciously transmitted and always unconsciously received. An underthought, though subtle, can undermine the message of the overthought. Northrop Frye, the Canadian literary critic, quoted as an example the scene in *Henry V* where the Archbishop is blessing the English army as it embarks for France. His overthought is of victory, conquest and glory. The underthought is carried in the imagery of sunken ships and lost treasure. That's a negative example. Hopkins never mentions positive underthoughts but (presumably) they're close to what are here called 'undertones' – unconscious forces (instress?) which maker the bearer grow and mature.

Hopkins was born in 1844 in Stratford, now in the East End of London, then a village by the river. His family, a big one, was staunchly Anglican, and so was he. His father, a loss-adjustor with Lloyds of London, was also a part time poet, author of actuarial books, consul-general for Hawaii, and well enough known to have been asked to write a review of *In Memoriam* for *The Times*. When the family moved to Hampstead in 1852 to escape the creep of London, the young Hopkins was sent as a boarder to Highgate School where in the following century John Betjeman was taught by T S Eliot (the man who wanted to be a mystic but never quite made it).

Oxford in the 1860s was still partially embroiled in the Tractarian Movement and he was drawn to Catholicism largely by the example of Newman, a fellow-mystic and a fellow former Anglican. When he was twenty-two Hopkins converted, to the dismay of his family, and was received into the Church by Newman himself. (He taught for a term or two at the school attached to Newman's Oratory.) The following year Hopkins went even further and a became a novice in the Society of Jesus with Newman's encouragement, it seems. The rest of his life, twenty-two years of it, was bound up in study, Ignatian Exercises and contemplation, teaching, and spells as a curate. His jobs took him to Oxford, Chesterfield, Sheffield, Glasgow, Manchester, Liverpool, Manresa House (the Jesuit HQ in Roehampton), Stonyhurst, and above all – for his poetry at least – St Beuno's College near St Asaph in Flintshire. Most of his nature poetry was written in a single year (1877) in the Vale of Clwyd's great green and airy bowl with views of the mountains of Snowdonia in the West, and in the valley of the River Elwy.

He seems to have been a misfit even with the Jesuits – as a parish priest his sermons might have gone down better with theologians than the labourers who were his parishioners in Liverpool or Sheffield – and his Superiors didn't know what to do with him. Then they found his niche – Professor of Latin and Greek in Dublin's University College (which, curiously enough, Newman had set up in 1851). Yet this, too, backfired. As a Fellow of the Royal University of Ireland he was the country's Greek and Latin examiner, marking up to thirty thousand papers a year. He was short, slight, over-sensitive and very English, quite wrong for a country where England was detested and for a workload he was too conscientious to shirk. He seems to have over-worked himself (particularly in marking exam papers) and may have weakened his immune system. Whatever the reason, he died of typhoid fever in 1889, just before his forty-fifth birthday.

Hopkins, it's also fair to say, was a profoundly introverted man; reality for him was an inner one, and his inner space was filled with the Divine which, being a Christian priest, he called God or Christ or the Holy Spirit. In November,1881, he was still in Manresa House near Richmond Park after taking his final vows. He wrote to Canon Dixon, his old Highgate schoolmaster: "My mind is here more at peace than it has ever been and I would gladly live all my life ... in as great or a greater seclusion from the world and be busied only with God." That certainly sounds like the authentic introvert who's found his inner life's companion. He was then thirty-seven.

He burned his poetry when he became a novice at the age of twenty-four because he thought he had no right to it unless sanctioned by his superiors. That sanction came in 1875 when the Rector of St Beuno's asked him to write a poem about the loss of the steamship, *Deutschland*, wrecked in a snow storm on the Kentish Knock in the Thames estuary just before Christmas. Among her passengers were five Franciscan nuns exiled from Germany by the Lutheran anti-Catholic Falck laws. For over thirty hours, the ship lay stranded on the sand bank, beam on to the sea and the storm. Her lower decks flooded. Men were ordered into the rigging, women and children on to table tops in the first class saloon. Hopkins, in Wales, read the story in *The Times*. All five nuns died, but not before one of them had a vision of Christ walking on the sea. His poem – called *The Wreck of the Deutschland* and written in his new tough and sinuous Sprung Rhythm – was rejected by the Jesuits' magazine, *The Month*.

All the same, he now had permission and he used it to write verse for his remaining fourteen years – around forty-six major pieces in total. Some of his work can be difficult – he's a one-off but not impenetrable (or *unthoroughfaresome*): a crib get you through it easily. It falls into three phases. First came the mystical nature sonnets written at St Beuno's in 1877. In the second phase he wrote chiefly about people and his work is more priestly with a sadness and a pity for humanity rather than rapture. The last phase,1885-9, included the Terrible Sonnets. Four of them, he said "came like inspirations, unbidden and against my will." The four, it's thought (he never specified) are: *Carrion Comfort, No worst there is none, I wake and feel the fell of dark, and To seem the stranger lies my lot.*

For low level mystics the poetry of the first and third phase are the important ones. Caught in them is joy in the Other-World and the desolation of disconnection from it.

In *The Windhover* the poet-mystic is on the hills above the great bowl of the Vale of Clwyd just after dawn (we know the exact day: 30th May 1877) when his eye is caught by a hovering kestrel (windhover, in dialect). He watches as the kestrel rides the air as though it were a solid like ice (with a skater) or a riding ring for horses. Precision and grace is here. The sight – the mastery, splendour, and earthly perfection – shuts down the poet's mind when, all at once, the flight of the kestrel buckles as she stoops; the mind of the watching man – and in turn the mind of the reader – buckles too to let in Eternity, portrayed (because the poet was a Christian priest) as Christ. But *everything* on earth leads to this conclusion – from the sheen of the ploughshare polished by soil to burnt-out blue-bleak embers which break open into a gold-vermilion Beyond.

Pied Beauty was also written at St Beuno's, where he was reading theology, in the summer of 1877. It's a 'curtal' sonnet, one of his own inventions (and words), coming in at ten and a half lines, in a ratio of 6:4 (and a half). *Pied Beauty* really is about the particularity of things: it's a list of inscapes, followed by the instress (God) which makes them. Each is like a lid; lift it and look at the Lord. Praise Him, also, because that's what mankind was born to do, according to the Jesuits at any rate. God's love should be given back instantly, Hopkins believed.

Glory be to God for dappled things -
For skies of couple-colour as a brinded cow;
For rose-moles all in stipple upon trout that swim;
Fresh-firecoal chestnut falls; finches' wings;
Landscape plotted and pieced – fold, fallow, and
   plough;
All all trades, their gear and tackle and trim.

All things counter, original, spare, strange;
Whatever is fickle, freckled (who knows how?)
With swift, slow; sweet, sour; adazzle, dim;
He fathers-forth whose beauty is past change:
Praise him.

Hurrahing in Harvest is an even purer example of mid-to-low level mysticism. It came out of a half-hour event as he walked home, alone, from a fishing trip to the River Elwy on the first day of September, 1877.

> I walk, I lift up, lift up heart, eyes,
> Down all that glory in the heavens to glean our saviour;
> And, eyes, heart, what looks, what lips yet gave you a
> Rapturous love's greeting of realer, of rounder replies?

The Terrible Sonnets record what happens to an introverted mind when the inner world is disconnected from the Beyond (or God, as Hopkins perceived it) and collapses. These sonnets are the most graphic, most accurate, and therefore the most harrowing, of any in English dealing with the desolation of this disconnection. To anybody who has ever been there, and escaped, they bring back the torment/torture/searing agony of those endless nights when grief threatened to stop the heart as it beat too loudly, too hard, and the brain itself felt on the edge of bursting, physically, open. At times like those, verses like these are a comfort of a kind; a sharing of suffering, perhaps, as in the sad brotherhood of *The City of Dreadful Night*.

> I wake and feel the fell of dark, not day.
> What hours, O what black hours we have spent
> This night! what sights you, heart, saw; ways you went!
> And more must, in yet longer light's delay.
> With witness I speak this. But where I say
> Hours I mean years, mean life. And my lament
> Is cries countless, cries like dead letters sent
> To dearest him that lives alas! away
>
> I am gall, I am heartburn. God's most deep decree
> Bitter would have me taste: my taste was me;
> Bones built in me, flesh filled, blood brimmed the
>   curse.
> Selfyeast of spirit a dull dough sours. I see
> The lost are like this, and their scourge to be
> As I am mine, their sweating selves; but worse.

Even in his pain, Hopkins hit on the cause of his distress: the absence of the Other because of thoughts (an endless carousel of thought) about the self. The lost *are* like this. The lost are this. The self is dysfunctional because it's no longer what it should be: it's unselved by self-absorption, and the gateway to God (as Hopkins would have seen it) is locked shut. No-thought opens the way to the Heaven. Thought closes it. Self-absorbed thought opens the way to Hell.

Total disconnection didn't last long – only from the winter of 1884/5 until, possibly, early next year. Three years later he wrote one of the world's longest sonnets with the world's longest title: *That Nature is a Heraclitean Fire and of the Comfort of the Resurrection*. It begins with a long lament that entropy will do for us all, people and things alike, in time. Then comes the comfort of the Resurrection : "I am all at once what Christ is ... This Jack, joke, poor potsherd, patch, matchwood, immortal diamond/Is immortal diamond."

Hopkins also had a mystic's take on beauty and the aesthetics of good manners. Beauty shows people the inner nature of things and opens up insights into goodness and grace. In 1879 he was serving as the stand-in priest in the church of St Aloysius in Oxford. That Easter a ten year old boy helped him in the Sacristy. What could he buy him as a thank-you gift? "What you buy me I like best," the boy said. Hopkins was so taken by the mannerliness, the graciousness, of the reply that he wrote a poem about it. He called the boy 'handsome of heart' and 'mannerly-hearted'. The best gift, he decided, was to pray he never lost his 'handsome heart', by which he meant beauty of character, something far greater than beauty of body or of mind. Mannerliness of heart, like good manners, is aesthetic. It radiates undertones (and underthoughts), adding something of value to the world. Mannerliness and insight together form a benign feedback loop. More than that, mannerliness is like a conduit; grace flow along it. It's like a pipeline from the Beyond. The Beyond is thus penetrable or *thoroughfaresome*.

The Curious Case of the Missed Connection

The curious thing about Matthew Arnold (1822-1888) is that he skirted round and round mysticism, knew its causes and its effects, but never quite got there himself. He sensed that thought was the problem, and non-thought the answer, but was never able to stop thinking. It was as though he had the wires in his hands but never touched them together to let the power flow.

You can see how close he got to the answer in *Empedocles on Etna* which he wrote in 1849 when he was only twenty-seven. (He was still only twenty-nine when he wrote *Dover Beach*, that enduring lament for lost faith.) *Empedocles* is a short narrative poem; short on narrative, long on argument. Of the three characters, one is invented, two were historical. Empedocles himself is the pre-Socratic philosopher who said that everything is made of earth, air, fire, and water. The mixing is done on a cosmic scale by Love and Strife which are invisible yet obvious (people quarrel and fall in love). In the poem Empedocles is (or was: he's lost his power) a miracle-worker who could calm the storm and cure old age. In reality he didn't die on Etna, although an under-sea volcano off the coast of Sicily is named after him. Pausanias, his companion, was also an historical figure. In real life he'd been Empedocles's catamite, as was the custom in Antiquity. Callicles, the harpist and bard, is invented although his songs are based on Pindar and Ovid.

The story is simple. The Greek colonies in Italy are unsettled by Sophistry, the philosophy which says anything goes – half lies, lies, deceit, statistics – as long as you win, which is defined as closing down the argument: there's no such thing as truth, only a victor and a silenced opposition. Empedocles can take this corruption no more and sets off to kill himself in the volcano. Pausanias goes with him part of the way – for his own ends as much as anything else. Callicles is part of the plot for one reason only – to illustrate a better way of looking at things. His ideas border on the minor mystical, but don't cross it because Arnold himself never got beyond that frontier.

A sub-theme of wet and dry, arid and fertile, shade and sun runs through the whole poem. Callicles stays hidden in woods by the rivers of the lower slopes. Empedocles climbs across the cindery-dry pumice through harsh sunlight to the cone of the volcano where he kills himself in the heat of the crater. This imagery, of course, underlines a right and a wrong way of looking at life.

Four philosophies are broached. Pausanias is an extravert and an externalist – everything that happens to people is caused by events outside themselves. (Both Callicles and Empedocles disagree; the answer is almost always within.) Pausanias thinks that Empedocles had once been able to raise the dead. If he could find out how, he too could defy the gods and live free of fear forever.

Empedocles has two things to say to him, and the first is meant as a gift, as wages, to pay Pausanias for his service and help him live without his master's company. People's problems are caused by limited understanding and vision, he begins. (Souls are like mirrors swinging on strings; they see in part and in snatches.) Because we can see only piecemeal doesn't mean there isn't a meaningful whole. People invented gods because they needed something to blame for the mess they make of their lives. The need for happiness is wired in, but nobody has a right to it. Unhappiness is caused by the mismatch of what people want and what they have. Youth wants rapture and chases it. But life is short and, when they don't find it, they look to an afterlife to give it to them. People waste their lives waiting for death. Everything – gods, cosmos, people – is made of the same material: how can you hate what you're made of? Is living with love and sunlight so small a thing that you long for death? All you can do is make the most of what you have, and don't despair.

146

But Empedocles no longer lives by this philosophy himself. When he's alone on the rim of the crater, we learn what he truly thinks. Philosophy and thought are a hindrance and get in the way of truth. Mind and thought are wrong for this world. Thinkers are aliens. The reason seems to be a mystical one: thought blocks access to the Under-Reality, the All.

But for Empedocles there's another snag: he's a reincarnationist who believes the same troubles will follow him through life after life in an eternity of time. All he can do is stop the pain of this particular life by killing himself. He jumps into the white hot lava of the crater. In those few moments of free-fall, thought stops and (we assume) he's in touch with the Under-Reality and the All. We assume because Arnold doesn't say, and Arnold didn't say because he didn't know.

Meanwhile, Callicles feels Etna heave and watches the flames flare as Empedocles is burned up. Immediately afterwards he sees Apollo and the Nine Muses ("their garments out-glistening/The gold-flower'd broom") as they stop to swim in a pool before going to their home on Olympus. They glorify the Creator, they glorify the nature of things, glorify the peace of the immortals, they glorify ...

> The day in his hotness,
> The strife in the palm;
> The night in her silence,
> The stars in their calm.

Apollo, of course, is the god of light and clarity, music and intellect. The two can be combined. Callicles, an artist, instinctively knows the secret which eludes the thinking man: salvation comes through art and the daily miracle of common things. If Callicles knew it, so did Arnold – but only intellectually, not as a living experience.

In *Stanzas from the Grande Chartreuse* (written between 1851 and '55) Arnold says he is:

> Wandering between two worlds, one dead,
> The other powerless to be born.

For him that other world always was to be unborn, but he had no right to speak for anybody else: for some it never died, and still hasn't. At the end of the poem he apologises to the 'master of the mind': he wasn't making friends with Alpine monks, he explains – he was merely a sightseer looking at two dead faiths, his and theirs. But of course the monks' faith wasn't dead and it took a certain kind of insolence and arrogance to suggest it was. Especially as for the next forty years he searched for that unborn world, hoping to find it in Culture, Hellenism, poetry, or creativity. He never did. For many people that new world has never been born, either, probably because there's no substitute for a variant on the old one.

Yet for all his misconnections, he has a lot to offer the mystically inclined; some of his poetry is good enough for word-mysticism and is often full of undertones. What he uncovered in his search is useful too: he took over from Newman, who took over from Coleridge, and put together ideas which influenced English society until very recently. To begin with, he coined the phrase "the best of what's been thought and said" to sum up what kind of knowledge should stock the well-filled mind. What he couldn't say – and yet which seems to be a fact – is that this well-lit mind is needed for spiritual entelechy. It's the ultimate undertone sustaining a sense of Ultimate Reality just underneath the level of consciousness, a kind of permanent sub-mystic experience. It's as though fullness approaches Fullness.

He was also like a colour blind man who's painted a picture in an almost perfect combination of colours which he can't see, but others can. It was as though there was a membrane, just a little too thick for osmosis, between Arnold and the spiritual. *The Scholar Gipsy* is one of the few poems which is set in his own country, which may account for a lot. Some have called these verses the last in a line of pastoral poetry which began with Virgil, and there is something 18th century about them, influenced as they were by Gray's *Elegy*. All the same, this is not a pastoral – it's a quest poem. As such it fails because Arnold didn't know what he was looking for, and failed to recognise it when he found it.

As an undergraduate in the 1840s Arnold often walked on the Cumnor Hills with his friend Arthur Clough. *Thyrsis* and *The Scholar Gipsy* are set there. He found the story, which is apparently true, in Joseph Glanvil's *The Vanity of Dogmatising* (1661). A student of Oxford, too poor to pay his way, joins a band of gipsies to learn how to control other people's minds (although control of his own was all he needed). Arnold soon forgets this, however, and the scholar-turned-gipsy becomes a listless wanderer on the Cumnor Hills and Berkshire Downs, passively waiting for a 'spark from heaven'.

Whole stanzas create undertones. If they're read when young, they'll still be working when old. Some can calm the mind to a point, not where the mystic moment breaks through, but where it's sensed on the periphery vision. Some verses, in other words, let Meaning as well as meaning sidle in.

> But when the fields are still,
> And the tired men and dogs all gone to rest,
> And only the white sheep are sometimes seen
> Cross and recross the strips of moon-blanch'd green,
> Come, shepherd, and again begin the quest!

And:

> While to my ear from uplands far away
> The bleating of the folded flocks is borne,
> With distant cries of reapers in the corn -
> All the live murmur of a summer's day.

And:

> And air-swept lindens yield
> Their scent, and rustle down their perfumed showers
> Of bloom on the grass where I am laid,
> And bower me from the August sun with shade;
> And the eye travels down to Oxford's towers.

And:

149

Moor'd to the cool bank in the summer-heats,
'Mid wide grass meadows which the sunshine fills,
And watch the warm, green-muffled Cumner Hills,
And wonder if thou haunt'st their shy retreats.

Arnold's life as a poet was short: ten years, maybe, between his early twenties and thirties. In this he's like Wordsworth although, unlike him, Arnold gave up on poetry almost completely. He then married a judge's daughter, became an inspector of schools, set up as a thinker and set about changing the English through thought. His argument was with the Dissenting middle classes – shopkeepers, manufacturers, counting house clerks, chapel preachers – who lived in drab intellectual, aesthetic and spiritual poverty, trapped by self-deceiving smugness. Industrialism was not the cause – their cast of mind dated back to the 17th century Puritans. By their narrowness and aloofness from their own civilisation they diminished themselves and everybody else. (Their other vice was addiction to liberty – 'freedom is a good horse but where are you riding it?') (Today their descendants have the same cast of mind but a different mindset.)

The odd thing is he was aware of what he called 'the Eternal not ourselves'. Others might associate this with the divine. Not Arnold. To him it makes people righteous, and nothing more. All his life he confused the spiritual with rectitude, mistaking priests for policemen with moral truncheons. Religion shackled the Old Adam and for that reason alone was worth keeping, but only if he could filter out the impossible and the superstitious – opium for the masses, perhaps, without the high. (Robert Bridges called him Mr Kidglove Cocksure.) In the 1870s, with the help of literary criticism, he set about saving Christianity by stripping out the religion while leaving (as he thought) moral usefulness behind – a bit like a tone deaf man keeping the orchestra but stopping it making all that appalling noise.

God is only a metaphor for something glimpsed at the edge of consciousness. The Bible is poetry. Theologians had hardened its poetic fuzziness and fluidity into something too concrete. As a text it responds like any other to the critic's basic question: "what does this *do*?" Calvin was a poor critic who misread it. Calvinism was based on reason and reason is not the basis of religion. Arnold saw that far but no farther. Again there's something here of Newman's thoughts on the Bible and change.

At heart Arnold was an intellectual, an ideas man. The ideas which appealed were French, and abstract. More than that he was a natural born statist before there was statism, a 20th century man in a 19th century world. Few statists are mystics, mild or otherwise. What the mystic sees can't be collectivised, controlled, counted, banned or taxed and re-distributed equally among all. Arnold was a home grown social engineer and bureaucrat of limited vision.

The Socratic question "how should we live?" was fundamental to him, and was a moral one. His answer was through 'Culture': or an overview of the highest that civilisation has of offer, "the best of what's been thought and said" in his own words (he had a gift for the apt and snappy saying). With it we overcome narrowness and bigotry to see the world steadily and see it whole, as Sophocles did. Culture is active, working away unseen inside us. A critical mass of knowledge can change people for the better. (His concept of Culture was narrowly literary, and very Newmanian.)

He was also aware of the unconscious, its importance and power. His concept of 'disinterestedness' has a Zen feel to it. By it he may have meant Newman's 'implicit reasoning' – let the unconscious solve problems free from the emotional tangles and snarl-ups of the upper mind. Don't, for example, look for the meaning of art: leave it to the unconscious which will (presumably, although Arnold never said so) turn it into an undertone to expand, change and evolve you.

Art, also, should 'animate and ennoble'. To Arnold, poetry was so powerful that he thought it would in time replace religion. Poetry works, he thought, through beauty. The more beautiful, the greater the ennoblement. It changes us by overcoming despair and selfishness to makes life bearable. (Again he missed the deeper meaning of people like Burke, Wordsworth, Coleridge, or Newman.) He did realise however that good art should make you bigger and better and he himself rejected *Empedocles* because it diminishes the reader. (Browning got him to put it back in later editions of his work.) "What does it do for you?" he asked his friend Arthur Clough about *The Scholar Gipsy:* it was pleasantly melancholy but was that enough? Art had to be a transformer.

As well as Culture and Poetry, two other ideas shaped Arnold's world view. Hellenism to him meant radiance of thought and clarity of mind. Greekness was the antithesis of ugliness and ignorance. Grace and serenity were Greek. A life lived Greekly would be at ease in mental sunlight. This radiance, that grace and serenity, are undertones, the gift of Hellenism to the receptively minded.

Creativity was also vital. Under it he included learning and, criticism and even just doing anything well. Happiness is the outcome, and happiness is an indicator of deep genuineness, authenticity and truth, which is the mystic's point entirely.

Atheism didn't suit Arnold's temperament. Something was needed to fill the gap. As it was, isolation and loss defined him. He also seems to have been an introvert – one to whom the inner is more real than the outer. The thinking introvert searches for an overview or grand unified theory. Arnold did. (What was missing was the mystic gene.) The loneliness of the introvert was there also. In *To Marguerite – Continued*, a poem about the woman he never married, he says: "We mortal millions live *alone* in the sea of life en-isled." On summer evenings, each of us is alone on a mortal island and we despair as we sense that we were once part of the main. Why, then, are we now alone? Because a god decreed it. Between each of us now flows "the unplum'd, salt, estranging sea". Again, however, he's speaking for everybody without permission: the mildest of minor mystic senses that all islands are joined by land under the sea.

Another curious and inexplicable fact about Arnold is that he personally knew a mystic and a genius (or a mystical genius): Wordsworth. The Arnolds and the Wordsworths were neighbours in Westmorland. Arnold knew him in the flesh but not the spirit. Arnold mistook Wordsworth's joy for his own mild pleasure in the Cumnor Hills. On the other hand he did know these experiences came when Wordsworth was free of his lower self. To Arnold, Wordsworth's joy in nature was moral because it taught people how live. The fact that the joy was a spin-off, a by-product, was an insight to which he was himself blind. He saw the flame, not the fire.

We can, then, easily sum up Matthew Arnold, the near-miss mystic. He knew thought blocks something, but not what was blocked. Being unable to let go of self-consciousness was, he also knew, the problem. He experienced a sense of greaterness but linked it wrongly with uprightness, honesty and common decency. What some called God, he saw, could be glimpsed on the edge of consciousness. Aesthetics makes us bigger and better. Poetry almost certainly gave him what some others would call a religious experience. Wordsworth's insights, he realised, came when the lower self had been dropped. Above all, he knew that undertones of some kind rise out of Culture when it reaches a critical mass, but never realised they can be, for some at least, spiritual. He was a man who never joined up the dots, or made the right connections. Perhaps he expected a peal of tower bells when, usually, you get only the handheld kind.

But was he changing towards the end? He died in Liverpool of a heart attack at the age of sixty-six while waiting to meet his daughter on her way back from the United States. By then he'd lost three of his five children and perhaps age and loss had changed him in some way. In 1863, in *Spinoza and the Bible* he compared the intellectual life to the Christian one. In the latter you are transported by love, in the former by following the reasoning of Plato. Yet Plato very specifically says that both are ways to the same end – a meeting with The Good. However sixteen years later in his essay on *Byron* he recognised the value of Wordsworth's joy in nature as being "healthful and true." It's also moral because it shows us how to live. In fact, what we have is almost a formula: Joy + Healthfulness = Truth (J+H = T). Like $M=EC^2$, it can be reversed: $T = J + H$.

153

TWENTY

The Coral Hills of Cumnor

The Cumnor Hills as portrayed in *The Scholar Gipsy* are an Arnold-construct. The real ones are better, at least for people open to the mysticism of landscape. In many places in the world they'd barely register – five miles long, maybe, two and a half miles wide, five hundred and fifty feet high at the most. Not a place to spend several lifetimes wandering over as the scholar turned gipsy does in the poem. Five slightly higher points could be called peaks – Cumnor Hill, Hirst Hill (which are in line with each other) and Boar's Hill which is separated from them by a low saddle or col. Farther northwest are Beacon and Wytham Hills. The Cumnors are made of coral laid down in a tropical Jurassic sea a hundred and fifty million years ago, a fact which also partly explains why Oxford is where it is; the coral is so hard it forces the Thames into a loop – the city is on a bend in the river.

Outwardly – in places – the tops of the hills haven't changed too much since Arnold's day. Reapers in the corn have gone but corn still grows over the curve of the hill crests, yellow in late summer against the sky. The hedges are now tall with old gnarled trees. Elder, foxglove, guelder rose, convolvulus, dog daisies, cow parsley, shepherd's purse, campion are still common, with loosestrife, meadowsweet and bedstraw by the river. They're an old man's hills, silent save for the noise old ears brings with them, easy on the heart with gentle slopes and folds: 'fat' sums them up quite well, hard coral hills though in fact they are. There are no rivers, of course, only cress-hidden rills as described by Arnold in his poem.

154   The difference between poem and reality lies mainly in what Arnold cut out – in particular two villages along with their churches. Cumnor, which he never mentions, had a

population of a thousand in his day and still dominates the summit of the hills. In turn it's dominated by a solid church with a confident tower on its own hillock. St Michael's is 11th century in origin, 13th in construction. Did Arnold ever go inside? It has a serenity which comes only with time. In the nave you can hear the ticking of the clock in the tower. The last stroke of the hour echoes for a good thirty seconds before fading back into the deepest silence. The walls are so thick that the midday summer sun never reaches the floor but stays on the slope of the sills. You don't need to believe in anything to be enlarged by the mystery of a space which seems to abolish space itself, and time. It insists on nothing, although it feels like a connector between here and somewhere else (if there is such a place).

The etymology of Cumnor is unknown; 'Cuma's hillside', possibly, after an 8th century Abbot of Abingdon. The abbey owned the hills for centuries and in the 14th the monks built a big house called Cumnor Place as the abbot's summer residence (the Thames valley was notoriously sultry in summertime). After the Dissolution of the Monasteries the first secular owner was the last abbot. A few years later, Amy Dudley, wife of the Queen's favourite and future Earl of Leicester, was a tenant. In 1560 she was found dead at the foot of the stairs. Foul play? The authorities said not. The villagers thought otherwise: Amy's ghost is said to have haunted the hills for centuries until no fewer than nine Oxford vicars drowned her in the village pond which hasn't frozen over from that day to this. The story's told in Scott's *Kenilworth*. Cumnor's also the Lumsdon of Hardy's *Jude the Obscure*.

By Arnold's time seven thousand acres of the hills belonged to the Earls of Abingdon. In 1814, the 5th Earl, still in his mid-twenties, enclosed the land hereabouts thus creating the landscape in which Arnold placed the Scholar Gipsy who'd begun his wanderings on unenclosed hills a hundred and fifty years earlier. The Earl lived in Wytham House (renamed Abbey in 1850 for no known reason) at the foot of the escarpment at the western end of the range. Arnold razed that as well.

Arnold's at his most graphic in describing the river and the plain fringing the hills. The scenery around Bablock Hythe in particular won't have changed too much, though The Ferry Boat Inn is a new building with an unchanged name. A bell for calling the ferryman is still nailed to a willow. Today's ferry, like the old, is essentially a broad beamed punt. Back then, the ferryman hauled on an overhead rope made fast to either bank. Arnold has the Scholar Gipsy reclining in the ferry, trailing his hand in the water. This is unlikely: the gunwale was only a few inches high and the crossing couldn't have taken more than three or four minutes (the river really is a stripling here as Arnold says).

The mill on the Seacourt Stream was also unmissable, although missed out from the poem too. For a couple of miles, this little river flows very rapidly across the Wytham flats parallel to the Thames. A leat leads out of the stream and back to it in a loop. The mill and the miller's house stand on either side while the water wheel would have turned in between them. A stone bridge spans it, joining two great wooden barns which are now, like the house and mill, abandoned. Self-sewn willows grow everywhere in the damp soil.

It brings to mind Vaughan Williams's setting of a little known bit of verse by a little know Georgian poetess, Fredegond Shove. She was his first wife's niece, and bridesmaid, which may explain a few things, such why he bothered to set it to music in the first place. *The Water Mill* (1922) is about a very un-Chaucerian miller, his family, and cat.

> The miller's wife and his eldest girl
> Clean and cook while the mill wheels whirl...

> The young men come for his daughter's sake,
> But she never knows which one to take.

156

Arnold also eradicated Wytham, a winding village without a pond or a green, built of Oxfordshire stone and thatch. The inn is called the White Hart and probably has connections to Richard II whose badge it was. There's a dove cote, now birdless, but presumably alive in Arnold's day. The village, and the woods and hills behind, are now owned by the University and so are a bit lifeless and time-stopped but over the centuries the parish register records sawyers and millers, shoemakers and cowmen, shepherds and grooms, hurdle makers, butlers and coachmen (in the big house). In other words, the hills were more dynamic than Arnold allowed.

All Saints in Wytham at first sight looks Tudor with a stumpy tower not much higher than the roof, and a bright blue clock face with golden hands and gilded Roman numerals. It was built, in fact, in 1811 by the 26-year old 5th Earl to replace a ruinous church on the same spot. Partly it was built with material from the old church, partly of stones from Cumnor Place, which also sent down some stained glass. The faces in this glass are pure Queen Anne. Other figures in other windows are distinctively Victorian, pre-Raphaelite. In front of the first pew is a triangle of lead coloured organ pipes. Under the belfry is a grey painted gallery with a bright Royal Coat of Arms. The clock chimes tinnily. It's a thoroughly homely little place. Did Arnold not stand there in the silence and look at the corbels with the faces of a nun, a bagpiper, a playing-card king, a man in a mitre? The man in the mitre might even be the young Earl himself. (He was still alive, then in his sixties, when Arnold passed that way.) The hedge around the churchyard is draped in ivy and the grave stones are lichened into unreadability.

An Oxford Elegy

In the late 1940s Vaughan Williams set *The Scholar Gipsy* and *Thyrsis* to music as *An Oxford Elegy*. He cut and pasted them together to make a hybrid with the theme of waiting, not seeking, for a spark from heaven. "The light we sought is shining still" is the message extracted from the run-together poems.

Thyrsis was Arthur Hugh Clough (1819-1861), a friend of Arnold's from their university days, and one of his companions on walks over the Cumnor Hills. Like Arnold, Clough was a poet who became a bureaucrat. His poetry changed from the vainglorious to the cynical. From:

> Say not the struggle naught availeth,
> The labour and the wounds are vain,
> The enemy faint not nor faileth.

To:

> Thou shalt not steal; an empty feat
> When it's so lucrative to cheat

Thyrsis is his memorial. What action there is takes place on a single November afternoon. The poet/narrator takes the path to Childsworth Farm – now Chilsworth – on the northern slopes of Boar's Hill looking for the Signal Elm. If it lives, so does the Scholar Gips – and suddenly there it is, stark against the sky and therefore "Our Scholar travels yet the loved hill-side". A very strange non-conclusion you might think. Clough was dead: if there are any answers, he'd know them; if there's nothing to be known, there'd be no Clough to know. Arnold, in fact, had nothing to say. Perhaps he was being badgered by Clough's widow to write a memorial for her husband (it was written three or four years after his death). The result is more laboured than *The Scholar Gipsy*, more reliant on second hand mythology though in places it has the edge when it comes to local colour.

> So have I heard the cuckoo's parting cry,
> From the wet field, through the vext garden-trees,
> Come with the volleying rain and tossing breeze:
> The bloom is gone, and with the bloom go I!

Arnold was was not a mystic. Vaughan Williams was. Arnold, however, could summon up that experience in others. Can Vaughan Williams? Not in *An Oxford Elegy* he can't. *The Scholar Gipsy* works because of its poetry of landscape. All that is lost in *An Oxford Elegy* which doesn't

158

evoke the curved, greened-over coral of the Cumnor Hills at all. It's peculiar too in being spoken, not sung, which may be a mistake, particularly if the actor declaims, which they tend to do. What happens in the only winter scene in *The Scholar Gipsy* is an example. The scholar turned gipsy crosses the flood plain and climbs to the crest through the snow and ...

> ... gain'd the white brow of the Cumner range;
> Turn'd once to watch, while thick the snowflakes fall,

The narrator now leaves a gap for a flutter of violins before declaiming ..

> The line of festal light in Christ-Church hall.

It doesn't work. Apart from anything else the gap means the speaker will get the intonation wrong: it should be a dying fall but can't be. The words themselves, and the imagery, are undertones and a 'magic casement' in their own right. Cluttering it up and breaking it does, in fact, break it. As it is, the whole piece is a bit too linear with music awkwardly wrapped around words or playing for long stretches by itself. Words and music often seem uncomfortable together and are a poor fit where they fit at all.

In fairness it has to be said *An Oxford Elegy* made at least one man weep at its première in Cambridge in 1952. On the other hand, Steurt Wilson, the man who wept, was the reader: perhaps the words made him cry.

Binsey Poplars

It's a pity Hopkins never wrote poetry about the Cumnor Hills. All we have are some note book entries – notable for his eye for colour – and *Binsey Poplars* which is set in sight of the hills but on the river bank below them. Hopkins lived in Oxford twice, once as an undergraduate, once as a priest.

The 3rd of May, 1866, was a cold, raw and wet morning followed by a bright afternoon when the sky turned "sleepy blue without liquidity". The twenty-two year old Hopkins with his friend Addis crossed the river by the ferry at Bablock

Hythe and went by Skinner's Weir to the Witney Road. That afternoon they stood on the Cumnor Hills looking down on Oxford, being just able to pick out the spire of St Philip's through "the blue haze rising pale in a pink light." The hills were "just fleeced with grain".

The top of the hill to their left (Wytham Hill? Now wooded?) was "glistening with very bright newly turned sods and a scarf of vivid green slanting away beyond the skyline against which the clouds shewed the slightest tinge of rose or purple." Buds were just breaking on the oaks and elms though not the ash. White poplars were "most beautiful in small grey crisp spray-like leaf." If May sounds late for trees to be still in bud, it should be remembered that the Little Ice Age had nearly twenty years to run before the climate in England began warming, before dipping again around 1940 (and climbing again in the 1970s).

Back down by the Thames that day Hopkins noted the "green water of the river passing the slums of the town, and under its bridges swallows shooting, blue and purple above and shewing their amber-tinged breasts reflected in the water, their flight unsteady with wagging wings and leaning first to one side then the other. Peewits flying,"

Thirteen years later he again walked by the river, as a priest this time. In a letter, dated 13th March 1879, to Canon Dixon he said: "I have been up to Godstow this afternoon. I am sorry to say that the aspens that lined the river are everywhere felled". Out of it came *Binsey Poplars*, a lament for the destruction of nature.

> O if we but knew what we do
> When we delve or hew -
> Hack and rack the growing green!
> Since country is so tender
> To touch, her being so slender,
> That, like this sleek and seeing ball
> But a prick will make no eye at all,

Binsey is a hamlet – or more correctly three houses and a pub called *The Perch* – thirty or forty yards from the river. *The*

Perch is old and small, still with a wood fire in the open hearth in winter, and piled up with logs. Back then it was possibly a jerry selling beer and ale to watermen and reapers. The immediate area can't have changed too much visually; the modern sprawl of Oxford, across the river and the Port Meadow, is out of sight behind trees. The aspens at Binsey, it turned out, were old and rotten and the farmer who owned them went on to plant saplings in their place. Perhaps the saplings are still there, now fully grown (ready for felling and replacing again?)?

All the same Hopkins grieved because the loss of natural beauty matters. Through it you meet God. Lose beauty and you lose an avenue to the Divine. But in this case the beauty is in the words, rather than any image they call up. Sound here creates an undertone of its own.

> My aspens dear, whose airy cages quelled
> Quelled or quenched in leaves the leaping sun,
> All felled, felled, are all felled;
> Of a fresh and following folded rank
> Not spared, not one
> That dandled a sandalled
> Shadow that swam or sank
> On meadow and river and wind-wandering weed-
> winding bank.

TWENTY-ONE

The Age of Umber?

Art to Ruskin, before politics and madness overtook him, was spiritual. Without the one you can't have the other. Worse, without both there can be no great society. Art, the embodiments of a culture, shows a society's greatness, or decay. Was he right? English history has two great literary and two great overtly mystical centuries. Do they coincide? The literary centuries are the 17th and 19th; the 19th and 14th are the mystical ones.

The 14th century wasn't entirely barren from a literary point of view – no period containing Chaucer could be. It was also pre-printing and a time of competing dialects. Chaucer and Gower spoke the East Midlands dialect from which today's English descends. Langland spoke the dialect of the River Severn valley. The author of *Sir Gawain and the Green Knight* was from the North Midlands (possibly Staffordshire) and the poet who lamented the loss of his daughter in the poem called Pearl was perhaps from Lancashire.

Then there were the mystic writers. Richard Rolle, author of *The Fire of Love*, had been a student in Oxford before becoming a hermit in the South Riding. He preached a religion of love, a reaction against Scholasticism. (His 'vision', paradoxically, was aural: he heard it as music. Bodily heat – calor – was also part of it.) Water Hilton, an Augustinian monk and canon lawyer from Nottinghamshire, wrote *The Scale of Perfection. Scale* is from the Latin for ladder or stairs: the book is about how to climb up to God through the myrkness or murk or darkness of sin. *The Cloud of Unknowing* was one of a group of five books, by an unknown author, teaching the techniques of contemplation – how to reach 'onehede' with God – after the manner of Richard of St Victor, the monastery in Paris. It was written for quiet nuns.

162

Margery Kempe's 'mystical crying', on the other hand, sounds like religious hysteria. Above all there was Julian of Norwich and her *Showings*. More importantly, Wycliffe also began translating the Bible into English from the Latin of the Vulgate.

William Langland's *Piers Ploughman* is the story of a soul in search of truth which, needless to say, is eventually found inside the mind where it's been all along.

> If grace grant thee to go in this wise
> Thou shalt see in thyself Truth sit in thine heart
> In a chain of charity as thou a child were.

It's a mystic's conclusion. (Charity of, course, has the old meaning of 'love' from the Latin *caritas*.)

All in all, then, quite a literary century especially when compared to the following one. The 15th was not only a literary wasteland (Hoccleve in verse, Malory in prose) but also a time when the language was in flux. It was the century of the Great Vowel Change when 'i', for example, evolved from the long Continental way of speaking to its present day shortness. For thirty years in the second half of the century the Wars of the Roses dominated the country. Malory, a knight of the shire of Warwick (probably) fought for both sides, spent time in prison, and was said to have been (among other things) a rapist, rustler, burglar, and Member of Parliament. Caxton printed the first book in English in 1473 (in Bruges).

The 16/17th century was, from the literary point of view, very great (given the presence of Shakespeare, the greatest). The number of mystics was relatively small but on the other hand it was an extremely religious age. The new Protestantism generated fervour and people like Drake were driven by it. The Civil Wars were partly religious, partly political, and ended in politico-religious dictatorship.

George Fox (1624-1691), the first Quaker, was the century's most outstanding mystic in that he founded a sect which is still around albeit with its spirituality diluted almost to the secular. Thomas Traherne (1636-1674) was a country parson near Leominster who lost his childhood vision and set about re-finding it by becoming like a child again, living on and bread, and water and ten pounds a year. He was a high level mystic whose vision was more vivid than that of the lesser run-of-the-mill kind. "The dust and stones of the street were as precious as gold…. Boys and girls tumbling in the street were moving jewels… The city seemed to stand in Eden, or to be built in Heaven." " The world is a mirror of infinite beauty."

Henry Vaughan (1622-16950 – mystic, poet and medical doctor – is known for one or two stanzas such as:

> I saw Eternity the other night,
> Like a great ring of pure and endless light,
> All calm, as it was bright.

The Cambridge Platonists – Cudworth, Whichcote, Culverwel, Smith and More – were Divines at Emmanuel who realised there are two Gods in Christianity – Jehovah and Plato's. They chose Plato's and looked for daily revelation through simplicity, honesty, sobriety and the Candle of the Lord. Their clotted prose is unreadable today. Marvell may have been a minor mystic. Donne wasn't one at all. Nor, probably, was George Herbert.

Yet there's more to it than that. Mysticism at all its levels is a sensing of a Greaterness and it doesn't have to be supernatural: patriotism can be a stand-in and the 16/17th century had that in plenty. There was also the matter of the Renaissance which came late to England – lasting about fifty years evenly divided on either side of the turn of the century. On top of that, of course, there was enormous native talent: Spenser, Shakespeare, Donne, Marlowe, Milton (who grew up in the last half of the English Renaissance). Four things, then, came together; talent, new ideas, patriotism, and religion.

Caroline Spurgeon also says that Platonism was fashionable in the Renaissance – even Puritans like Spenser could be drawn to it. It was a kind of fake mysticism, purely intellectual. One give-away was its disgust with the material world. All the same, there was a consciousness of a need to reach upward.

Very probably the 17th century's religious extremism led to Locke's Empiricism, the philosophy of doubt and therefore tolerance which was central to English thought until very recently. The 18th century, the Age of Reason, which was based on it, was a mystic desert. There were really only four mystics, well-known ones at least. Bishop Berkeley's mysticism was so pure that he failed to see how material reality could really be real at all. Matter exists only in a mind; when the human mind is absence, God's isn't. William Law is now unread and unreadable. Reading a sentence at random tells you why: "Fire uncreated, uncompacted, unseparated form the Light and Air, is the heavenly Fire of Eternity: Fire kindled in any material Thing is only Fire breaking out of its created, compacted state." Only two 18th century mystics have had a lasting importance. Burke began a strand of Toryism and John Wesley's Methodism helped shape the Labour Party at the end of the 19th century.

Dryden, a purely 17th century figure (he died in 1700), wrote modern prose for the first time and it was then written, with instant skill, by the generation which spilled over into Queen Anne's reign – Swift, Defoe, Addison, Steele. Later came Fielding, Sterne, Smollet, Goldsmith, Sheridan, Gibbon. And the Great Cham himself, Sam Johnson – an undertone in his own right. He was a devout Anglican Tory and completely unmystical.

It was a great age – the *first* age in fact – of the novel. Novelists and playwrights tend to be extraverts and, if mysticism is mainly a product of introversion, you wouldn't expect to find too many mystics writing fiction. Even the century's standard verse form, the heroic couplet, is stately and formal. Pope used it for philosophy ("Whatever is, is right" he tells us in *An Essay on Man*) as did Johnson in *The Vanity of Human Wishes*, a translation of Juvenal. Also, compare Cowper (1731-1800) on the wreck of the *Royal George* ("Toll for the Brave! The brave that are no more") and

Hopkins on the loss of the *Eurydice* ("*The Eurydice* – it concerned thee, O Lord"). Or *Binsey Poplars* with Cowper's "The poplars are fell'd! farewell to the shade/And the whispering sound of the cool colonnade." All the same, Gray's regular iambs had Romanticist themes (wild-haired bards and Odin) and the century ended with mystic writers (Blake, Coleridge, Wordsworth) crossing over into the new one.

Ruskin was wrong about his own times. The 19th century, he thought, had lost any sense of a world animated by the divine and the result was an Age of Umber, of spiritual and therefore of cultural darkness. Yet the 19th was a great century whose creativity of course spilled over into the early 20th. The 19th century had religion, it had mystics galore, it had patriotism, and it was endlessly dynamic and confident, an age of self-belief and culturally creative. People still live in its dying aftermath. It was also a cross-over century. If we're reading Thomas Hughes correctly, patriotism was beginning to falter. Religion was definitely losing its way and being replaced, not by Arnold's Culture, but by politics, by a rather rootless secularism, and by welfarism. In 1862, in *Unto This Last*, Ruskin set out the ideas which, forty-five years after his death, became the Welfare State. (Three mystics – Burke, Wesley, Ruskin – were therefore somewhere at the bottom of two opposing English views of life – left v right, Tory v Labour; the butterfly effect in motion, perhaps.) In 1867, Marx published *Das Kapital*.

All in all there does *seem* to be a correlation between art and the spiritual which, at the very least, is worth thinking about.

And today? By the middle of the 20th century the last of the Victorians were in middle or old age. Their qualities, whatever they were, may have been sapped by the Second World War – something certainly died around that time and in the late 1950s the Great Discontinuity came along, an abrupt rupture with history. The past – and its sense of Greaterness – is no longer a living thing. People who were adult when the Great Split happened now live in a country

166

different from the one they were born into – a lesson in how to become an alien without a change of address.

Quakers illustrate the new world and the new mood nicely. Fox's Society of Friends was all about the spiritual. Central to it is the concept of the Inner Light which is clearly a kind of lesser mysticism. At their weekly Meetings there's a centring down into silence. If that quietness leads to an emptying of minds, it can of course let in the Inner Light and all that follows. At the same time, people who are moved to speak can do so. Nowadays – instructively – what people are mostly moved to speak about is left wing politics. A Quaker meeting is like listening to the letter page of *The Guardian* being read out aloud, at length, in full. You can't have a collective Inner Light; it goes out like a candle, leaving a trail of smoke and smugness.

So is the early 21st century Ruskin's Age of Umber? Minor mystics instinctively think so – the idea resonates with what they are. But if, as argued here, mysticism is often a factor of introversion, then by definition a mystic's understanding of the outer world is likely to be flawed or wrong. The touchstone, as always, is the Ruskinian one: "Does this make us bigger and better?" A lot of art in England today is consistent with hate, envy, spite, and a discontent and resentment masquerading as social consciousness. It's a literature generating few undertones, and mostly negative ones at that. In many ways it's the art of darkness, a kind of anti-art which diminishes and decreases people, and also fully matches Ruskin's belief that the art of his own time was one of anxiety, a malaise. Nobody can claim this is a time of greatness. It's an Age of Smallness, if not of Umber. Yet greater and weaker times seem to come and go, each a century long, like breathing in and out. If there is a pattern, then the later 21st century should be spiritually and therefore culturally rich – unless, that is, the West is already in terminal decline.

Bibliography

TWO: *Encounters of a Lesser Kind*

Happold, F C. *Mysticism: A Study and an Anthology*. Penguin Books. London, 1984

Masefield, John. *The Oxford Book of English Mystical Verse*. Oxford University Press. Oxford, 1917

Masefield. John. *Sea-Fever; Selected Poems of John Masefield*. ed. Philip W Errington. Carcanet Press. Manchester, 2005

Masefield, John. *Sea Life in Nelson's Time*. Sphere Books. London, 1972.

THREE: *Mild Mysticism and Change*

Craig, David M. *John Ruskin and the Ethics of Consumption*. University of Virginia Press. Charlottesville, 2006

Landow, George P. *The Aesthetics and Critical Theories of John Ruskin*. Princeton University Press. Princeton, 1971

Landow, George P. Ruskin. *Past Masters*. Oxford, 1985

Ruskin, John. *Modern Painters*, ed. and abridged David Barrie. Pilkington Press. London, 2000.

Ruskin, John. *On Art and Life*. Penguin Books. London,

Ruskin, John. *The Lamp of Beauty, Writings on Art by John Ruskin*. selected and edited by Joan Evans. Phaidon. Oxford, 1959

Ruskin, John. *Unto This Last and Other Writings*. Penguin Books, London, 1985

FOUR: *Ruskin: Romsey Abbey and the Renaissance*
Romsey Abbey. The Pitkin Guide. Andover, 2008

FIVE: *The Vale of the White Horse*

Chesterton, Gilbert Keith. *Poems for All Purposes*. London. Pimlico, 1994

Hughes, Thomas, *The Scouring of the White Horse*. Boston. Ticknor and Fields, 1859.

Hughes, Thomas, *Tom Brown's Schooldays*. Electronic version from Project Gutenberg produced by Gil Jaysmith and David Widger.

SIX: *The Undertones of Patriotism*

Kipling, Rudyard. *Puck of Pook's Hill*. Penguin. London. 1987

Kipling, Rudyard. *Rewards and Fairies*. Wordsworth Classics. Ware, Hertfordshire. 1999

Kipling, Rudyard. *Selected Stories*. Penguin Books. London. 2001

Orwell, George. *The Collected Essays, Journalism and Letters, Volume 2, 1940-1943.* Penguin. London. 1984
www. dewponds . com

SEVEN: *A Valley of Vision and the Lonely Tower*
Anderston, Anne; Meyrick, Robert; Nahum, Peter. *Ancient Landscapes and Pastoral Visions.* ACC. Woodbridge, 2008
Grigson, Geoffrey. *Samuel Palmer: The Visionary Years.* London, 1947.
Lister, Raymond. *The Paintings of Samuel Palmer.* Cambridge University Press. Cambridge, 1985
Vaughan, William, Elizabeth E. Barker, and Clive Harrison. *Samuel Palmer, 1805-1881: Vision and Landscape.* Lund Humphries, London,2005.
Paintings:
Coming from Evening Church. Tate Britain, London.
The Magic Apple Tree. FitzWilliam Museum, Cambridge
In a Shoreham Garden. Victoria and Albert Museum, London
Study of a Garden at Tintern. Ashmolean Museum, Oxford
The Black Waterfall, near Dolgelly. Courtauld, London.
Pistyll Mawaddach, North Wales. Tate Britain, London.
Tintagel Castle, Approaching Rain. Ashmolean Museum, Oxford
A Dream in the Apennine, Tate Britain, London.
Opening the Fold. Private Collection.
The Lonely Tower (watercolour), Yale Center for British Art, New Haven
The Lonely Tower (etching). Private Collection.

EIGHT: *Music and the Common Mystic*
Kennedy, Michael. *The Works of Ralph Vaughan Williams* (2nd Ed). Clarendon Press. Oxford, 1992
Vaughan Williams, Ralph. *Vaughan Williams on Music.* ed. David Manning. Oxford University Press. Oxford. 2008
Vaughan Williams, Ursula. R.V.W. *A Biography of Ralph Vaughan Williams.* Clarendon Press. Oxford, 1964

NINE: *Kado: The Way of Words*
Benson, A C. *Edward FitzGerald.* MacMillan. London. 1905.
Blyth, R H. *Haiku* Volumes 1-4. The Hokuseido Press. Tokyo, 1982-4
Blyth, R H. *A History of Haiku* Volumes 1-2. The Hokuseido Press. Tokyo, 1984
Blyth, R H. *Zen in English Libterature and Oriental Classics.* The Hokuseido Press. Tokyo, 1942
Eliot, T S. *Collected Poems* 1909-1962. Faber & Faber. London, 1983
Hoff, Benjamin. *The Tao of Pooh.* Methuen, London, 1984
Kipling, Rudyard. *The Works of Rudyard Kipling.* The Wordsworth Poetry Library. Ware, 1994.

Marvell, Andrew. *Andrew Marvell*. Oxford University Press. Oxford, 1990.

Suzuki, D T. *Zen and Japanese Culture*. Princeton University Press. Princeton, 1973

Suzuki, D T *Studies in Zen*. Unwin. London, 1986

Suzuki, D T *Essays in Zen Buddhism*, Series I-III. Hutchinson, 1985

Suzuki, D T *An Introduction to Zen Buddhism*. ed. Christmas Humphreys, Foreword C G Jung. Hutchinson, 1983

Thomas, Dylan. *Collected Poems 1934-1953*. J M Dent & Sons. London, 1989

Yeats, W B. *W B Yeats Collected Poems*. MacMillan. London, 1984

TEN: *Miscellany: Science, Systems, Politics.*

Thomas, Edward. *Richard Jefferies*. London: Faber, 1978.

Chadwick, Henry. *Early Christian Thought and the Classical Tradition*. Clarendon Press. Oxford, 1992

Chadwick, Henry. *The Early Church*. Penguin Books. London, 1993

Dodds, E R. *Pagan and Christian in an Age of Anxiety*. W W Norton & Co. New York, 1970

Spurgeon, Caroline F E. *Mysticism and English Literature*. Cambridge University Press. Cambridge, 1913.

Burke, Edmund. *A Philosophical Enquiry into the Origin of our Ideas on the Sublime and Beautiful*, ed. Adam Phillips. Oxford University Press. Oxford. 1990

Burke, Edmund. *Reflections on the Revolution in France*. ed/introduction Conor Cruise O'Brien. Penguin Books. London, 1983

McCue, Jim. *Edmund Burke and Our Present Discontents*. The Claridge Press. London, 1997

Popper, Karl. *The Open Society and Its Enemies*. Routledge. London, 1971.

Turner's *Snow Storm – Steam Boat off a Harbour's Mouth*. Tate Gallery (Turner Bequest), London.

ELEVEN: *A Long Defeat and a Failure*

Adams, Edwin William. *Memoirs of a Social Atom*. Hutchinson. London, 1903.

Burton, Robert. *The Anatomy of Melancholy*. Clarendon Press/Oxford University Press. Oxford, 1989-94

Leonard, Tom. *Places of the Mind: the Life and Works of James Thomson (BV)*. Jonathan Cape. London 1993.

Ridler, Anne. *Poems and Some Letters of James Thomson*. Southern Illinois University Press. Carbondale, 1963

Salt, H S. *The Life of James Thomson (BV)*. Reeves and Turner. London, 1889

Thomson, James. *The City of Dreadful Night*. Watts & Co. London, 1932

Eliot, T S. *The Complete Poems and Plays*. Faber. London 1969

Eliot, T S. *Notes Towards the Definition of Culture*. Faber. London, 1979

Eliot, T S. *The Sacred Wood*. Methuen. London, 1964

TWELVE: *Adolescent Undertones?*

The Application of Thought to Criticism ed. John Carter CUP. Cambridge, 1961

Housman, A E. *Collected Poems* (Introduction by John Sparrow) Penguin. London, 1956

Housman, A E: *A Collection of Critical Essays* ed. Christopher Ricks Englewood Cliffs NJ: Prentice Hall 1968

Housman, A E. *Introductory Lecture* 1892. Cambridge University Press. Cambridge, 1937

Housman. A E. *The Name and Nature of Poetry*. CUP 1933

Housman, A E. *Selected Prose*. Cambridge University Press. Cambridge, 1961

Orwell, George. *Inside the Whale (Collected Essays, Journalism and Letters Vol 3. 1943-1945)*. Penguin. London, 1984

Page, Norman. *A E Housman: A Critical Biography*. MacMillan. London, 1996

THIRTEEN: *The Mystic Century*

Spurgeon, Caroline F E. *Mysticism and English Literature*. Cambridge University Press. Cambridge, 1913.

Thompson, Francis. *Selected Poems*. Burns and Oates. London, 1908

FOURTEEN: *The Minor Mystic's Manual*

Darbishire, Helen. *The Poet Wordsworth*. Clarendon Press. Oxford, 1966

Purkis, John. *A Preface to Wordsworth*. Longman. London, 1987

Wordsworth, William. *A Choice of Wordsworth's Verse*. Selected with an Introduction by R S Thomas. Faber and Faber. London, 1971

Wordsworth, William. *The Letters of William Wordsworth*. ed Alan G Hill. Oxford University Press. Oxford, 1990

Wordsworth, William. *The Prelude 1799, 1805, 1850*, W W Norton. New York, 1979

Wordsworth, William. *The Prelude: A Parallel Text*. ed J C Maxwell. Penguin Books. London, 1986

Wordsworth, William. *Wordsworth Poetical Works*. Oxford University Press. Oxford, 1985

FIFTEEN: *The Thinking Mystic's Mariner*

Coleridge, Samuel Taylor. *Biographia Literaria*. J M Dent & Co., London, 1908

Coleridge, Samuel Taylor. *The Golden Book of Coleridge*. J M Dent & Co. London, 1909

Coleridge, Samuel Taylor. *The Portable Coleridge*. Ed./introduction by I A Richards. Penguin Books. London, 1981

Coleridge, Samuel Taylor and Wordsworth, William. *Lyrical Ballads 1798*. ed. W J B Owen. Oxford University Press. Oxford, 1991

Holmes, Richard. *Coleridge*. Past Masters. Oxford University Press. Oxford. 1982

Wordsworth, Dorothy. *Journals of Dorothy Wordsworth*. ed Mary Moorman. Oxford University Press. Oxford,1987

Wordsworth, Dorothy. *Letters of Dorothy Wordsworth, A Selection* ed. Alan G Hill. Oxford University Press. Oxford, 1982

SIXTEEN: *The Cardinal and the Clerisy*

DeLaura ,David J. *Hebrew and Hellene in Victoria Literature: Newman, Arnold and Pater*. University of Texas Press. Austin. 1969

Newman, John Henry. *An Essay in Aid of a Grammar of Assent*. ed. Ian T Ker. Oxford University Press. Oxford, 1985

John Henry Newman: *Prayers, Poems and Meditations*, selected and introduced by A N Wilson. SPCK, London, 2008

Newman, John Henry. *Apologia pro Vita Sua and Six Sermons*, ed. Frank M Turner. Yale University Press. New Haven, 2008

Newman, John Henry. *The Idea of a University*. Yale University Press. New Haven, 1996

Strange, Roderick. *John Henry Newman: a Mind Alive*. Darton, Longman, and Todd. London, 2008

SEVENTEEN: *The Second Mystic Laureate*

Martin, Robert Bernard. *Tennyson: The Unquiet Heart*. Faber. London, 1983

Tennyson, Alfred, Lord. *In Memoriam*. ed Robert H Ross. W W Norton. New York, 1973

Tennyson, Alfred, Lord. *Poems and Plays*. Oxford University Press. Oxford, 1991

EIGHTEEN: *Unthoroughfaresomeness*

Gerard Manley Hopkins, *A Critical Symposium*. F R Leavis et al. Burns and Oates. London, 1975

Hopkins, Gerard Manley. *The Major Poems*. ed Walford Davies. J M Dent & Co. London, 1979

Hopkins, Gerard Manley, *Poems and Prose of Gerald Manley Hopkins*. Selected with an Introduction and Notes by W H Gardner. Penguin Books. London, 1963

Hopkins, Gerard Manley. *Poetry and Prose*. ed Walford Davies. J M Dent & Co. London,1998

Hopkins, Gerard Manley. *Gerard Manley Hopkins*. ed. Catherine Phillips. Oxford University Press. Oxford, 1986

Hopkins, Gerard Manley. *Selected Letters*. ed Catherine Phillips. Oxford University Press. Oxford, 1991

Hopkins, Gerard Manley. *Selected Poems*. ed. Dr Peter Feeney. Oxford University Press. Oxford, 1994

Hopkins, Gerard Manley. *Selected Prose*. ed. Gerald Roberts. Oxford University Press. Oxford, 1980

Mackenzie, Norman H. *A Reader's Guide to Gerard Manley Hopkins*. Thames and Hudson. London, 1981

NINETEEN: *The Curious Case of the Missed Connection*

Allott, Kenneth. *Matthew Arnold*. Longmans Green. London, 1968

Collini, Stefan. *Arnold*. Oxford University Press. Oxford. 1988

Arnold, Matthew. *The Complete Poems*. ed. Kenneth and Miriam Allott. Longman. London. 1987.

Arnold, Matthew. *Poetry and Criticism*. ed. A Dwight Culler. Houghton Mifflin Company. Boston. 1961

Arnold, Matthew. *Selected Poems and Prose*. ed. Miriam Allott. Dent. London, 1978

Arnold, Matthew. *Selected Prose*. ed. P J Keating. Penguin Books. London, 1970.

DeLaura ,David J. *Hebrew and Hellene in Victoria Literature: Newman, Arnold and Pater*. University of Texas Press. Austin. 1969

Eliot, T S. *Selected Essays*, Faber and Faber. London, 1980

TWENTY: *The Coral Hills of Cumnor Cumnor*

Evans, R J W. *St Michael's Cumnor*. The Church Publishers. Thanet, 2008

Graves, Robert. *Collected Writings on Poetry*, ed. Paul O'Prey. Carcanet Press. Manchester, 1995

Sparks, Margaret. *The Parish of Wytham*. Available from The Village Stores, Wytham. 2008

TWENTY-ONE: *The Age of Umber?*

The Cloud of Unknowing. a new paraphrase by Halcyon Backhouse. Hodder and Stoughton. London, 1992

Hylton, Walter. *The Scale of Perfection*. ed. Halcyon Backhouse. Hodderf and Stoughton. London, 1992

Rolle, Richard. *The Fire of Love*. ed. Clifton Wolters. Penguin Books. London, 1981

Julian of Norwich Showings. trans. Edmund Colledge and James Walsh. Paulist Press. New York, 1978.

Law, William. *A Serious Call to a Devout and Holy Life and The Spirit of Love*. ed. Paul G Stanwood. SPCK. London, 1978

Index

A

Abingdon, Earls of 155, 157.
Achili Affair 124.
Addison, Joseph 26, 165. Works:
The Spectator 26.
Aesthetic Movement 25.
Age of Reason 26, 108, 165.
Age of Umber 22, 25,162, 166.
Agnosticism 11, 51, 127, 131.
Aitken, Conrad 83.
Anglicanism 44, 74, 84, 99, 109,
110, 122, 123, 139, 165.
The Ancients 39, 40.
Alps 20, 21, 104, 147, 148.
Apollo 147.
Aquinas, St Thomas 138.
Aristotle 46, 57, 68, 118.
Arnold, Matthew 24, 68, 108, 109,
111, 120, 122, **145-153**, 154, 155,
156, 157. Works: *Byron* 153.
Empedocles on Etna 152. *Dover
Beach* 145. *The Scholar Gipsy* 54,
79, 148, 149, 152, 155-159. *Spinoza
and the Bible* 153. *Stanzas from
the Grand Chartreuse* 148. *Thyrsis*
149, 157, 158. *To Marguerite -
Continued* 152. (See also *An
Oxford Elegy*.)
Arnold, Dr Thomas 108.
Art for Art's Sake 25.
Arts and Crafts Movement 25.
Associationism 103, 118.
Atheism 22, 152.
Atlantis 17, 18.
Auden, W H 31, 69, 84.
aware 60.
Avalon 132.

B

Badon, Battle of 32.
Barnes, William 136.
Basho 60, 61.
Bax, Arnold 88.
Being/Becoming 21.
The Beggar's Opera 51.
Benson, E F 63. Works: *Edward
Fitzgerald* 63.
Beowulf 135, 137.
Berkeley, Bishop 165.
Berkshire Downs 149.
Berthon, Rev. E L 27, 28.
Betjeman, John 31, 139.
The Bible 23, 24, 71, 95, 124, 131,
150, 151, 153, 163.
Birmingham Festival 127.
Birmingham Oratory 124, 140.
Blake, William 16, 39, 66, 68, 72-
73, 90-91, 93, 166. Works:
Auguries of Innocence 91. *The
Everlasting Gospel* 91. *Holy
Thursday* 91. *The Marriage of
Heaven and Hell* 91, 92. *May
God us keep* 66. *A Vision of the
Last Judgement* 72.
Bliss, Sir Arthur 88.
Blyth, R H 59, 60, 61. Works: *A
History of Haiku* 59.
Boehme 19.
Border ballads 137.
Bradlaugh, Charles 76, 77.
Bridges, Robert 135, 150.
Brontë, Emily 90, 92. Works: *The
Prisoner* 92. *Wuthering Heights*
92.
Brooke, Rupert 30, 31, 90. Works:
The Soldier 30, 31.
Browning, Elizabeth Barrett 90,
93. Works: *Aurora Leigh 93.*
Browning, Robert 16, 90, 93, 94,
152. Works: *The Ring and the
Book* 93.
Buchan, John 15, 19, 90. Works:
Memory Hold-the-Door 15.

181